MORE>
Trust
Giving our dreams to
the trustworthy one.

Leah McFall

FORM

First published in Great Britain in 2021

Form
36 Causton Street
London SW1P 4ST
www.spck.org.uk

Copyright acknowledgements can be found on p. 115.

British Library Cataloguing-in-Publication Data
A catalogue record for this book is available from the British Library

ISBN 978–0–281–08456–2
eBook ISBN 978–0–281–08457–9

Typeset by CRB Associates, Potterhanworth, Lincolnshire
First printed in Great Britain by Ashford Colour Press
Subsequently digitally printed in Great Britain

eBook by CRB Associates, Potterhanworth, Lincolnshire

Produced on paper from sustainable sources.

Contents

iv   About the author

v   Introduction

1   Chapter one: (Re)learning to trust

9   Chapter two: Trusting through pain

19   Chapter three: Dreaming with trust

31   Chapter four: Trusting through fear

45   Chapter five: Trusting in the desert

63   Chapter six: Plans not to harm you

85   Chapter seven: Trusting your identity

99   Chapter eight: Trusting God with your future

114   Bibliography

115   Copyright acknowledgements

About the author

Leah McFall is a Northern Irish singer-songwriter. She rose to fame after finishing as runner-up on the second series of the BBC series *The Voice*. She has since toured with will.i.am, Jessie J and Ghetts, and sung at MusiCares grammy event in honour of Carole King, sharing the stage with Lady Gaga, Pink and Alicia Keys. The singer went on to write, record and release her independent EPs *INK* and *White X*, which not only became iTunes album chart toppers and secured Spotify editorial playlistings but also sold out her five-city UK independent tour. She frequently leads worship and speaks at Christian conferences such as with Hillsong and LST. She contributed to *Fearfully Made* by Carlos Darby and Hillsong. *MORE>Trust* is her first independent book.

Introduction

Do you remember when you were a child and you would do a 'trust fall' with your friends? No? Then you probably had very interesting toys. A 'trust fall' is basically where you ask a friend to stand with his or her back facing you before falling back into your arms, all the while trusting that you will catch him or her. This was a serious game. It tested and sometimes ended friendships. Nothing hurt your heart more in the playground than if your best friend didn't have enough **faith** in you to plummet back into your loving little bony arms. And if you weren't **brave** enough to **risk** bone breakage by falling back into your friend's loving little bony arms, you were left with unbearable **shame**. (Mind you, not as much shame as playing 'catchy kisses' for a solid seven years of primary school and never actually being chased for a kiss. Not a single one.) The thing is, as a child, you probably always did it. You fell and fully trusted that you would be caught. And yet, over the years, something began to change.

Five years ago, when my husband and I started dating, we went for a walk. He always makes up little games and he wanted me to stand on a three-foot-high wall and fall back into his arms. When I wisely refused, he was jokingly offended and said, 'You don't trust me.' The truth is, he is a complete messer and I absolutely did *not* trust him to catch me. Still, as an adult I will likely never participate in that game again. Why? Because I'm older and wiser? Because I don't feel like playing any more?

No. It's because I've fallen and got hurt too many times.

As children I think we instinctively trust. We trust our parents to protect us, to love us. We trust teachers to tell us the truth. We trust friends to be there for ever. We trust our dreams will come true. We trust God. And it isn't until our trust is broken for the first time and we get hurt that we become more cautious and selective with it. Maybe as adults we need to **relearn** how to wholly trust again. But not with just anyone. In fact, I would argue that only one being is worthy of that childlike, blind, unquestionable, falling-fully-into-your-arms kind of trust. God. Why? Because God **cannot** and **will not** ever break it. But having trust in God takes **faith**. It takes being **brave**. It means taking **risks**, and sometimes we find it **shameful** to admit we are struggling to trust him.

Where are you on the trust spectrum with God right now?

Imagine God physically standing behind you, asking you to fall back into his arms because he will catch you. Would you do it? Probably. I mean, he's God. He is perfect. And although in every painting I've ever seen of Jesus he looks a bit wafer thin, I am sure his catch is pretty good. But reflecting on your journey in life – the hurts, the disappointments, the unanswered prayers, the feelings of unprotectedness, the dreams still unfulfilled, that path you took believing it to be God-anointed only to come to a dead end rendering you completely lost – would you come to him with a new, fresh dream and immediately plummet back into his arms with it? Or would you be more hesitant this time, afraid he would let you fall to the ground and you would once again be left hurt and embarrassed?

Perhaps recently you have reasoned, 'Maybe he's teaching me a lesson,' or, 'He's testing my character,' or, 'God's timing isn't my timing,' when really, if you were to be truthful with yourself, you are starting to lose faith that he even exists at all, let alone is to be trusted. And maybe you've started to think that the world is right after all and you would be better off taking that dream into your own hands, 'just doing you', working hard and stepping over absolutely everyone and everything to make sure it comes true so that you never have the regret of what could have been. Your happiness is in your own hands, and choosing to trust your heart, and all the dreams and treasures within it, to a God you cannot see is utter insanity.

I have had these thoughts too.

I have had them to the point where, when I was asked to write this book a few years ago, I almost laughed in the lovely girl's face. I honestly felt I was the last person who should write a book on fully trusting God when I knew it had become my biggest struggle in life.

But throughout the Bible, God uses the broken to speak to the heartbroken. I love how he uses those still in the race to encourage others. He so perfectly loves the imperfect that he desires to meet them in the dirt.

God also meets us in the Bible. If we're struggling with trusting God, we're often not confident in hearing his voice. But the Bible is one of the key ways God chooses to talk to us, so we're going to turn to it often in exploring the trustworthy character of the Faithful One.

And so, with much humility and armed with the word, you have me talking to you about having more trust in God. Honestly, it is still my biggest struggle and my biggest desire in life. And I have had so many opportunities to forgo it completely.

You certainly don't need to pretend with me that you are at one end of the trust spectrum when truthfully you are at the other. Shame isn't from God, and there should be no shame in admitting we are struggling in this area. We are going to get honest in this book. We are going to be vulnerable. We are going to show the healer the deep wounds that we've tried to treat ourselves but are stinking of infection. We are going to be truthful with God if we blame him for inflicting those wounds or for allowing them to happen to us. He longs for us to come to him as we are, honestly and openly, so that he can give us a rest period while he gets on with restoring, healing and doing all the work for us.

What an awesome God we have. May he give us wisdom that will restore our childlike trust in him again.

God, draw close to us.

You see the state of our hearts. You see our desire to trust you that battles with our desire to self-protect. Help us to abandon pretence so that you can meet us where we are. Heal our wounds from falls in the past and teach us more about trusting you in our future.

Amen.

Remain in me, and I will remain in you. For a branch cannot produce fruit if it is severed from the vine, and you cannot be fruitful unless you remain in me. I am the vine; you are the branches. Those who remain in me, and I in them, will produce much fruit. For apart from me you can do nothing.

(John 15.4–5)

Chapter one

(RE)LEARNING TO TRUST

If, like me, you grew up in a loving Christian home, then you were probably taught from a very young age that God is to be trusted. I have loved God since I was a little girl. It was a real relationship even back then. I loved him as my heavenly Father, and if I could draw a picture of what my faith in him looked like, it would be of a little girl reaching up and holding her dad's hand while they walked a path together. She points at things, gets distracted, wants to sit, wants to perform for him, gets a bit huffy at times, falls down a lot, *but loves to do it all with him especially.* He picks her up, delights in her performances, laughs when she plays, comforts her when she cries, *and loves to do it all with her especially.* I trusted in my heavenly Father as wholly as I trusted in my earthly father. Which was 100 per cent.

Both my parents taught my sister and me Scripture from when we were toddlers. They taught us that we were intentionally created by a loving God and they taught us how to show God's love through the example of how they lived their lives, generously giving to others. Our little family was close – singing songs together on the way to our holidays, cuddling up on the sofa to watch *Gladiators* on a Saturday night, going to church together every Sunday – and yet our home was always open to people and we had a constant flow of church youth groups through our doors.

When I was 14, my parents came up to me in my bedroom, sat me down on the bed and told me they were separating. Although I had known that my dad was struggling in areas of his own life and had not been going to church for a few years by this point, I had not expected this and was absolutely heartbroken, as any child in this situation would be. This was the first time in my life where my security was being shattered and I started to blame God.

I felt abandoned and let down, and one night, on one of my many nights of telling God off, I told him that since he had promised me he had 'plans to prosper . . . and not to harm' me (Jeremiah 29.11, NIV), and he had not kept this promise, then I couldn't trust him any more and was going to live my life without him. Clearly, I was having a massive tantrum.

I don't advocate picking up your Bible, demanding that God speak to you and then opening a random page without reading the context surrounding a particular section, but on this night

I did exactly that. And I came across this scripture in John 15.4–5:

> Remain in me, and I will remain in you. For a branch cannot produce fruit if it is severed from the vine, and you cannot be fruitful unless you remain in me.
>
> I am the vine; you are the branches. Those who remain in me, and I in them, will produce much fruit. For apart from me you can do nothing.

STAYING IN THE VINE

These words were spoken by Jesus when he was preaching to his disciples before his arrest and crucifixion. He was trying to explain that he himself was the source of all life. A vine is a lifeline for a branch to flourish; it is where food and water are drawn up to nurture and keep the branches alive so that they can grow the fruit. A branch can fall off and die, but the rest of the plant survives.

Jesus is telling us here that we are a part of something bigger. We are the branches that God so desires to lovingly refresh with nourishment so that we can continue to bear fruit for others to benefit from. At a time when people were looking for the meaning of life in all the wrong places (and, let's face it, our culture is still doing this more than 2,000 years on), Jesus made it clear that a life rooted in your maker, feeding off his word and drinking in his truth, is the true meaning of life.

For me personally, I felt this was a direct answer from God asking me to not give up on him, that he wanted me to remain in him so that he could consistently feed me with truth, love, encouragement and strength. It is a simple scripture in many ways. Remaining in God does exactly what it says on the tin: it keeps you producing fruit and stops you from burning out.

I can say that in any season in my life where I have chosen, despite my circumstances, to remain in his Scriptures, praying and dwelling on him, that I have felt joy in pain, peace where there should be restlessness, and love and acceptance in the face of rejection. I suggest that within our first fall – where the security in our lives has been shattered and our childlike trust begins to waver – there is an immediate opportunity to relearn how to wholly trust in God again, and it begins by **choosing to remain in him**. Choosing to do something is so much more powerful than being conditioned to, and so much harder.

So, what does remaining in the vine look like?

For me, this scripture has been a rock to stand on. However, remaining in the vine has looked different in each changing season of my life. Sometimes I have reached the end of myself where I don't have the mental energy to do a three-hour Bible read or an hour-long prayer session. Some days, remaining in the vine has just been lying on my bed, listening to worship music and singing out words other people have written that I know I believe but feel incapable of coming up with myself. Sometimes it has looked like turning off my phone in the morning and being secluded in my uninterrupted time with God in his word.

For Jesus, staying connected to God the Father very often looked like retreating from the crowds and the busyness of life to have some time alone with God:

After he had dismissed them, he went up on a mountainside by himself to pray.
(Matthew 14.23, NIV)

He prioritized time to be refreshed and filled up by God before he poured himself back out again to fulfil his incredible purpose. I believe remaining in the vine is simply staying connected to God. Resting in his presence so we can keep getting refreshed. Not depending on our own strength so that we can thrive in his. Perhaps for now that doesn't mean demanding answers to questions or striving to be more disciplined. Maybe remaining in the vine for now looks like being still, knowing and trusting that he is God. As Psalm 46.10 (NIV) encourages us, 'Be still, and know that I am God; I will be exalted among the nations. I will be exalted in the earth.'

Whatever remaining in the vine looks like for you at the moment, it *is* this simple. Remaining in God is for your own good. It will keep you producing the fruits of the Spirit of love, joy, peace, patience, kindness, goodness, faithfulness, gentleness and self-control (Galatians 5.22–23).

REVISITING THE FALL

The breakdown of my parents' marriage was my first opportunity to forgo my trust in God. It was the first time I felt he had not caught me when I fell. The first time he had to ask me to choose to trust in him regardless of how I perceived my current circumstances, because he is faithful, good and worth remaining in. Whether we are learning to trust God for the first time or re-learning how to trust him, I think it is important to stop and reflect on the falls that have either left us with doubt about whether God is in fact trustworthy or convinced us that he isn't.

My mum always says that when you come out of a season you will be able to look back and say, 'What a way God brought me.' Perhaps, when you look back on the falls in your life, you need to ask God for healing. You need him to open your eyes to show you how he was there for you during that time because it still feels as if he abandoned you. Even though it can be hard, it is so important to look back with hindsight and see God at work in these places. Taking the time to reflect and remind yourself of how faithful he was in your past can provide much-needed encouragement to keep you trusting him with your future.

In the pages of the Old Testament, we see people building altars as memorials of when God had revealed himself to them or when he had caused them to be victorious. In Genesis, we see Jacob building an altar after God revealed himself to Jacob when he was fleeing from his brother Esau: 'Then come, let us go up to Bethel, where I will build an altar to God, who answered me in the day of my distress and who has been with me wherever I have gone' (Genesis 35.3, NIV). This altar would remind Jacob of how God was with him in the dark to restore hope.

Perhaps you could write out your falls in life, and if you feel God did reveal himself to you in those times, then make a mental altar of how God used each difficult time to carry you and reveal his heart towards you. Perhaps look back on old journals and insert a drawing of a pillar on these once dark moments in your life where God shone through.

Imagine yourself stuck in mud. All the heartbreaks and times of disappointment and broken promises have left your feet fully covered in a muddy, immobilizing cement of doubt. Looking back with fresh eyes on those times and seeing how God revealed part of his character to you and remained closer than you knew will allow you to exchange the doubting mud for pillars of trust and **free your feet**. Whether you're looking back on these experiences and can see God's hand in them clearly or you find yourself right in the middle of the storm, I promise you God has met me in my darkest moments and provided me with incredible scriptures to hold on to. And I am so glad he did, because learning to choose to rely on his strength during my first fall sustained me for my second.

Jesus wept.

(John 11.35, NIV)

Chapter two

TRUSTING THROUGH PAIN

As a child I always loved singing and performing, as did my sister Rebekah. We would make up dance routines and invite our parents in to watch. We sometimes even charged them an entry fee – savvy, business-minded children, eh?

My sister always believed in me; she encouraged me to join every contest going because she believed I would win. Even though she was three years older than me and should have been embarrassed when I came bursting into the living room in front of her teenage friends to perform Etta James's 'I Just Want to Make Love to You', she just laughed and asked me to do it again for Mum after they had left.

She was also one of the most caring people I knew. I had horrendous acne as a teenager; it made me cry a lot and I became very self-conscious. I would wake up at 3 a.m. to my sister sitting on my bed and applying spot cream to my face, trying not to wake me. She had set her alarm so that the cream could keep healing my skin all night rather than just rub off on the pillow. We fought and laughed together nearly every day. And after our parents' separation we clung to each other. We promised each other to always be close. To buy houses close to each other. To grow closer the older we got and to never let life get in the way.

It never occurred to me that death would.

On 31 January 2006, when I was 16 and my sister 19, I had not been able to get through to her on the phone all day. That evening the police arrived at our door. We were told that my sister had been in a car accident that afternoon and had died.

No warning. No time for a goodbye.

The days, weeks and months after the accident are a blur. I remember 'Time will heal' being spoken to me, along with, 'God wanted her home,' 'She'll always be with you,' and, 'No more days were written for her.' All these people meant well, and their words brought comfort later on but, at the time, if I'm honest, I hated those phrases. The biggest comfort I found during this time was that our house was constantly flooded with family, friends and people from our church who held our hands, wept with us, and said, 'This is not right.' Because it wasn't. I wept. My parents wept. The people who loved her wept.

'Jesus wept' (John 11.35, NIV).

QUESTIONS OF GRIEF

This was the biggest fall I've ever had. The biggest opportunity in my life so far to forgo my trust in God. He had the power to intervene, so why didn't he stop the van that drove into the car? Why did he allow this? How could I trust him with my dreams in life when he allowed such grief to devastate me? Was he even to be trusted at all?

Perhaps you have experienced something similar in your life and it has caused you to feel the same. And yet, despite my anger, I chose to remain in him, and during a situation at work I was prompted by the Holy Spirit to read a verse that would deepen my relationship with Jesus immensely.

A few years had passed since the accident and I was working part-time in a skin-care shop. I had become close to a colleague there who was absolutely hilarious, blunt and naturally cynical – the kinds of traits that solidify any of my friendships immediately. We would rarely have customers (because our products were offensively priced) and so would spend most of our shifts trying on the make-up we weren't selling and having deep conversations about life. Understandably, I was later fired from this job for talking a customer out of a £300 acne product that might as well have been yoghurt.

One day, about three hours into a shift, when our faces were caked about two inches thick, we started to discuss God. I knew she wasn't a Christian, but her issue wasn't believing *in* God, it was believing in a *good* God. She said to me, 'Leah, you are a good girl. And I have no doubt that your sister was just as lovely. So, if your God is so good, why did he let your sister die?'

At that exact moment a customer walked straight to my friend to ask for help. I've never been more grateful, because it felt as if someone had literally stabbed me. I immediately started praying, begging, 'God, you have promised to give me the words to say in these situations. I have no clue what to respond to her because, honestly, I don't know why you let her die. I'm angry that you did. But I *do* believe you to be good. Give me something to say to this girl. Please.' I kept remembering the verse 'Jesus wept', and was horrified because not only could I not remember what story in the Bible this verse belonged to, but it also had very little text to elaborate on because it was the shortest verse. Ever! But it was OK, because she'd been with this customer for a solid ten minutes so had most likely forgotten . . .

Nope! As soon as the customer left, she walked up to me and said, 'Well?'

I opened my mouth and started talking – *fast*. And *a lot*. I told her in detail that the world had been created by a good God and was good. But what is love without the decision to choose it? So, free will. So, an imperfect world. So, suffering and death. But *Jesus wept*. He meets us in our pain, comforts us and weeps with us. But that's not the end; he conquered death and will raise my sister back to life. I will see her again. What a **good** God!

Then my colleague said, with tears in her eyes, 'In my 40 years, I've never heard faith described like that.'

I laughed (with my five layers of mascara now dripping on to my chin) and said, 'I know . . . me neither.' And then I went home to read what my voice had just said.

Mary and Martha were heartbroken to have lost their brother. They had called for Jesus when Lazarus was ill, but he had not intervened in time and Lazarus had died. When Jesus came to them, he paused. And in the shortest verse in the Bible, one whose brevity causes us to pause on it, we read, 'Jesus wept' (John 11.35, NIV). Why did he do this?

The reason why we cry when someone dies and why we struggle to say the right thing when a person loses someone close to them is simple: death is not OK. It was never intended in God's original design for life. It doesn't sit well with us because it doesn't sit well with God. Death and grief do not come from him.

The verse 'Jesus wept' displays the compassion of our God. You've no doubt heard it said that Jesus became human and felt

Now a man named Lazarus was ill. He was from Bethany, the village of Mary and her sister Martha. (This Mary, whose brother Lazarus now lay ill, was the same one who poured perfume on the Lord and wiped his feet with her hair.) So the sisters sent word to Jesus, 'Lord, the one you love is ill.'

When he heard this, Jesus said, 'This illness will not end in death. No, it is for God's glory so that God's Son may be glorified through it.' Now Jesus loved Martha and her sister and Lazarus. So when he heard that Lazarus was ill, he stayed where he was two more days, and then he said to his disciples, 'Let us go back to Judea.'

. . . [Jesus] went on to tell them, 'Our friend Lazarus has fallen asleep; but I am going there to wake him up.'

His disciples replied, 'Lord, if he sleeps, he will get better.' Jesus had been speaking of his death, but his disciples thought he meant natural sleep.

So then he told them plainly, 'Lazarus is dead, and for your sake I am glad I was not there, so that you may believe. But let us go to him.'

(John 11.1–7, 11–15, NIV)

the full weight of all the emotions we have ever felt during his time on earth and therefore we can go to him about all things because he understands. That is true. However, I believe he goes further than this. I do not just believe 'Jesus wept'; I believe *he weeps still*. He is so deeply connected to our pain. I believe he understands our current loss not because he grieved a loved one, Lazarus, thousands of years ago. I believe he feels the weight of our hurt right now, in this moment, even more than we do.

The writer C. S. Lewis articulates this beautifully in his book *The Magician's Nephew*. In it, a little boy is crying at the feet of Aslan the lion about his sick mother. But when he looks at Aslan's face, he sees tears more wondrous than his own, and for a moment he feels as if Aslan is hurting about his sick mother more than he is. What a thought! God loves us and our loved ones more than we could ever hope to; we cannot understand the intensity of his heavenly and supernaturally fierce love for us. His heart breaks for us. This was not what he wanted for us. But he will bring good out of it because he is so entirely **good**.

Jesus lived. He was both fully human and fully God. He was there in the beginning when God created the world without sin and devoid of death. When Adam and Eve chose to disobey God and the earth began to fall away from God's original design, God watched generations of his people having to suffer in an imperfect world of heartbreak, pain and loss that the devil was now thriving in, and his heart broke, *just as it does now*. He came and met us in the dirt, *just as he does now.* He healed, he preached hope, he suffered for us. And when Mary and Martha grieved their brother, he went to them, paused and grieved *with* them. He died for us and he rose again to be with us here and now. In whatever season we are in.

I will always remember the love in our house during those awful months. The comfort of people who did not leave us to grieve alone. I believe God sends his church to surround people in their grief to show that he is there too, weeping and comforting us. That is how compassionate our God is! He never intended death, he did not cause the hurt and heartbreak that it creates in his world for his people, and yet he doesn't leave us alone to deal with it. And that is why I do not blame him for my sister's death.

However, that is not the end of the story. He did not leave it there.

Jesus called in a loud voice, 'Lazarus, come out!'
(John 11.43, NIV)

'I am the resurrection and the life. The one who believes in me will live, even though they die; and whoever lives by believing in me will never die.'
(John 11.25, NIV)

Jesus promised that Lazarus would be raised back to life, and he fulfilled that promise. The promise that death has been defeated through what Jesus Christ carried out on the cross is essential to our faith in God. He comforts us now and will resurrect us in the future. The promise that I will spend eternity with my sister who believed in Jesus is why I not only do not blame God for my sister's death, but I also praise and daily *choose* to trust him wholly with the rest of my life.

GRIEF IS LIFE LONG

Even as I write these words, 15 years on, the tears are dripping off my face on to the keypad, which I'm having to pat dry to continue. I do not know if you have ever experienced the grief of losing a loved one, but if you have, I am sure you would agree that it stays with you for ever. It catches you on a random day when it feels as though it happened yesterday. Your joy is always tinged with a little tug of the pain of loss. And though this pain can often cause us to question the trustworthiness of God, I now try to allow it to be a reminder of how God caught me.

In the peak of my grief, the incredible, life-giving hope we now have because of Jesus became the very air that I breathed, and I want it to be every day going forward. When I am frustrated at a promise from God that has not yet been fulfilled, I remember that it is because of him I will see my sister again. And if he is capable of that, then he is capable of all things.

The LORD told Joshua, 'Today I will begin to make you a great leader in the eyes of all the Israelites. They will know that I am with you, just as I was with Moses.'

(Joshua 3.7)

Chapter three

DREAMING WITH TRUST

Not only was I fortunate enough to grow up in a loving, Christian home that taught me I could trust God, but I was also encouraged to *dream* with God. I never doubted that I was designed and created by a Father in heaven who adored me and intentionally gifted me with things in my character that he delighted in seeing me use. I truly believed God would pave the way for all my dreams to come true, but discovering that things don't always pan out the way we imagine or expect is one lesson I need to learn time and time again.

I have always loved music. I never learnt how to crawl but was one of those creepy kids that 'bum-shuffled' everywhere. My parents tell me how all they would have to do was put Michael Jackson on in the living room and they would watch me speed down the corridor on my hands and bum to get to those 'jamons' calling my soul. My dad is also a singer, an extremely good one, and I watched him perform on various occasions and couldn't wait to one day be like him. That was probably where my love of music first developed. I sang *all* the time. And as I have mentioned, my sister and I sang, danced and made up shows together every day.

But I was a dreamer.

I was the kid who looked out of the car window on a rainy day and imagined I was in my own sad music video. I would listen to Mariah Carey's 'I Don't Wanna Cry' and position my face by a rolling raindrop so it would look like a tear on my imaginary camera. (I promise I had friends.) I was the kid who practised every Whitney Houston riff and was convinced that one day we would duet. My parents recall me telling God all about these dreams and asking him to just let Whitney know to wait on me because I was only six but I was pretty sure I would be available for said duet in around two years. I even remember saying to God, 'It's so exciting because I don't know at what age you are going to make me a pop star, but you do.' That's how sure I was of myself (clearly) and of the dream-giving and dream-fulfilling God I loved. I truly believe God delighted in seeing me, his little girl, curl up at his feet and hearing me thank him in advance because I *knew* he was going to make all my dreams come true.

As I grew up I worked hard on my craft. As a teenager I started singing in pubs all around Belfast and started writing my own songs. (Side note: I found my old notebooks full of lyrics I wrote as an emo teenager and, apparently, I used to write songs in Old English. 'I ponder down yonder' was legit one of my lyrics at age 14.) I led worship in church and had elderly ladies come up to me and say, 'Oh, love, your voice is beautiful. Keep it for the Lord; don't use it for that devil music.'

The thing is, the secular world was exactly where I intended to go. In my later teens I had come across the verse, 'I am sending you out as sheep among wolves. So be as shrewd as snakes and harmless as doves' (Matthew 10.16), and I felt my soul leap. I knew God was calling me into the world that rarely gives him glory. I asked my pastor whether it was wrong to not go into worship music, and he replied, 'Leah, only ever ask yourself, "Does where I am going need Jesus?" Then go!'

I moved to London when I was in my early twenties and started gigging all around music venues there. I had many seasons where doors were opening and then I would watch them shut one by one. Managers would be interested and promise to come to shows, then wouldn't show up. A&R from record labels (Artists and Repertoire division, responsible for talent casting) would email out of the blue after seeing one of my YouTube videos, only to never email back again. I would wait behind the security gates of management companies for someone to enter and then sneak in behind them to leave my demo. Then I would email them for months and months only to finally get a response asking me to stop contacting them as they weren't interested. But still, I kept going.

Until one day I got word that the reality television programme *The Voice* had seen my YouTube videos and were scouting for applicants. The record company in partnership with this show soon said to me, 'Your voice is like Marmite. The world will either love it or hate it. This show will let us know which one it is.' It felt as if it was the only way for me to move forward into the industry. I was frightened. I was afraid that by going on a reality TV show I would lose my credibility as an artist. I was afraid my family heartbreak would be exploited. I was afraid I would become famous but not have a career in singing; that I would be hated and be mocked across the national papers. I was afraid that I would be doing this alone.

Soon after I was approached, I attended my church, Hillsong London, and Christine Caine was speaking. (Christine founded the anti-human trafficking organization The A21 Campaign, and regularly speaks at Hillsong churches and conferences across the world.) She explained how she would often go into what she described as her 'cave' – uninterrupted time with God. She would turn off her phone and all distractions and spend time in the word and in prayer. I decided to do this. I asked God what book in the Bible he wanted me to read and my spirit felt urged to read Deuteronomy. I was, like, 'You sure, God? Not to criticize but I was kind of thinking of a Gospel, if I'm honest. No

offence, but sometimes the Old Testament is a bit of a bore . . .'
It turns out I was wrong.

REMEMBER GOD IN YOUR PLENTY

Reading Deuteronomy, which in turn led me on to the book of
Joshua, I discovered the story of the Israelites, who were rescued
from Egypt and rejoiced in their new-found freedom. And then
they walked into the desert and the fear that they had previously
faced returned. Then they conquered nations and were delivered
into the promised land. But then they forgot who had delivered
them there and so their forgetfulness bred disobedience.

As I read this story, God made my heart jump at certain verses,
prompting me to scribble them down in a little black notebook
that I would look at before every rehearsal. I had no idea then
why these verses were so important to me, but I do now.

I needed to remember that if I were to do well in a miraculous way, then I must be mindful of the God who performed
those miracles; God was the one I was dreaming with. He had
instructed that favour that would be on me while I was on the
show. He was the reason I hardly ever received any hate on-
line; the reason my social media seemed to triple compared to
that of others; the reason I had found favour among the executive
producers; the reason my cover of 'I Will Survive' charted in the
Top 10, breaking records at the time for a talent show contestant;
the reason I heard that I was signed the second I entered the live

When you have eaten your fill, be sure to praise the LORD your God for the good land he has given you.

But that is the time to be careful! Beware that in your plenty you do not forget the LORD your God and disobey his commands, regulations and decrees that I am giving you today. For when you have become full and prosperous . . . be careful! Do not become proud at that time and forget . . . that he led you through the great and terrifying wilderness with its poisonous snakes and scorpions . . . He did all this so you would never say to yourself, 'I have achieved this wealth with my own strength and energy.' Remember the LORD your God. He is the one who gives you power to be successful, in order to fulfil the covenant.

(Deuteronomy 8.10–15, 17–18)

performance, which usually doesn't happen; the reason a few of my truly awful performances on the show seemed to go unnoticed. And if you were to say, 'No. It's because of your talent that you did so well,' then I would ask you, 'And where do you think that talent came from?'

The problem I think many of us encounter when trusting God with our dreams is that we run ahead of him or forget to remember that it is he who is running the show. I truly believe God made a way for me to walk through *The Voice* in a way that would ensure I remembered his faithfulness to me and continued to obey him and trust his ways over the countless powerful presences that were about to enter my life.

I was so nervous before every show that I couldn't not cling to the word of God. I would drink hot water and honey repeatedly backstage while tuning out the humming and endless pacing of other performers, with worship music in my ears and scripture on my knees:

The LORD told Joshua, 'Today I will begin to make you a great leader in the eyes of all the Israelites. They will know that I am with you, just as I was with Moses.'

(Joshua 3.7)

If you are honoured, blessed in such a way that you are given favour above others, then keep in mind it is all for God's glory and not your own. How pointless to the kingdom would it be if it were for your own glory?! If you are to become a well-known church leader, an incredible worship leader or a leader in your creative industry, then make it so the world has to step back and say, 'God was with this person.' By giving God the spotlight on our stage, our dreams can become testimonies that could lead others to a life of knowing him.

I have been blessed with many highs in my career so far, highs that I share not to show off but so that you can better understand the reason I choose to love God more than my dreams. It can be too easy to seek to move on quickly from highs in pursuit of the next thing.

I came second on *The Voice* and was signed to Universal Records before I left. I was also pleased that, because I wasn't the winner, I was not obligated to release an album in a short time frame and instead could spend time writing with will.i.am in Los Angeles to make an original record. My dreams were absolutely coming true. I travelled to Los Angeles at the age of 24 and ended up staying for many months, completely on my own. But I didn't feel alone. I have never in my life felt so close to my God. I had clung to him on the show and prioritized my time with him even more than practice. It was a routine I got into because I felt so incredibly out of my depth. I felt so much like a 12-year-old girl and I *needed* my big God.

Before I knew it, I was in a studio called Record Plant where many legends had made their albums. Mariah Carey was in one room, Lady Gaga in another, Justin Bieber down the hall. I felt that I was in the right place. Will.i.am took me to parties where I met the top music business leaders in the world, and I was even politely asked by Dr Dre if I could move over as I was blocking the TV. I felt out of place all the time but had a constant conversation going on with God in my head 24/7. I shared a stage with Lady Gaga, Pink and Alicia Keys at a Grammy event. Tom Hanks came up to congratulate me on my performance (very kind considering it was the worst one I've ever done; still, I watched Tom Hanks films exclusively for the entire following year). I was asked to support Jessie J on tour and we sang a duet together. I was asked to tour with will.i.am and we sang many songs together all around Europe. I was making an album that I felt proud of and excited to share with the world.

For anyone looking in, I was living a childhood dream come true. And I was so thankful for the incredible experiences. Yet the goalposts kept moving. I wanted to release music I was proud of. I wanted an album release, not just a single. I think my biggest regret from this time, though, is that I didn't stop to enjoy it all. We sometimes forget to celebrate the wins because we've already moved on to the next battle.

In reality, my highs were never without the feeling of being unsafe – even my literal dreams were plagued with me appearing on a skyscraper, standing on a tiny bit of flooring, knowing that I was going to fall off. I had always prayed for wisdom and discernment in all my endeavours and I knew I would not be able to trust fully in the powerful business people who were demanding that I believe they had my best interests at heart. People who had no shared desire to give God the glory but instead demanded they were given the full credit.

I knew that it wasn't going to stay all 'up'. This was a journey.

I was starting to find friction between my wanting to glorify God with my career and how others wanted me to fulfil it. I was starting to get very frightened of where this was all going and who I was going to go with. Perhaps I knew in my spirit that it wasn't right for me. But regardless, I started to let the beautiful enjoyment of the blessings that God had given me be bludgeoned with large, black ink drops of fear and worry.

Perhaps you are in a season of highs right now and living your dreams. I think it is important to remind ourselves that God created joy and wants us to enjoy the blessings he has given us. The devil does not. God has already told us not to worry (Matthew 6.25–34). The devil *wants* us to worry. Please do enjoy the highs, so long as you always remember to thank God in your plenty and have a heart's desire for the world to see that it is because God is with you.

I also believe it is right to exercise discernment and to know when something is starting to not sit well with your spirit. Pray into it. Ask God for peace if you are in the right place, or to disturb your spirit enough to move you on if you are not. Ask him to give you the freedom to enjoy his blessings without spoiling them with your human desire to self-protect.

I am sending you out as sheep among wolves. So be as shrewd as snakes and harmless as doves.

(Matthew 10.16)

Chapter four

TRUSTING THROUGH FEAR

In 2020, the world was gripped with fear as a global pandemic made many of us think the outside world was now a zombie land. There had never been so many memes about the apocalypse. We hadn't received chain mail since 2002 but were now taking part in quickly forwarding an essay from a supposed doctor to our entire contact list. I remember taking my then three-month-old son out for our one allowed walk a day and seeing the empty streets, abandoned shops and the one person walking towards me, who had dared to cough about 30 seconds ago, just wishing I could engulf him back into the protection of my belly. The deadly virus was one thing, but the truth was, the pandemic of *fear* was everywhere.

Fears don't have to be universal to leave us immobilized. Fear can be completely personal and yet disturb our entire surroundings. I have felt fear many times in my career. Nerves gripping me before a performance. Worried I'm signing my life away in a contract and have trusted the wrong people to advise me. Terrified I'll make the wrong decision and miss out on the best opportunity of my life. Have you ever just woken in the night and thought through all the worst-case scenarios in your head, then carried them to the shower the next morning so you can have imaginary arguments in your head? Fear absolutely consumes us.

And what does God have to say about all this?

Proverbs 3.5–6 is a verse my spirit whispers over me every time I find myself gasping for air when fear is choking me: the thought that I am being led by the maker of earth and am not just fumbling around in the dark on my own.

Perhaps right now that isn't enough for you, or you are struggling to feel comforted by this thought just at the moment. I'll admit at times it has seemed strange to me that God would demand trust when I am afraid. Why doesn't he simply explain the fear away – silence my worry with an explanation of why he is allowing this all to happen or by telling me what is going to happen?

TRUST IN THE DARK

The truth is, God will always ask you to trust him in the dark before he invites you into the light. We see this throughout the

Trust in the Lord completely,
   and do not rely on your own opinions.
   With all your heart rely on him to
      guide you,
   and he will lead you in every decision
      you make.
Become intimate with him in whatever
      you do,
   and he will lead you wherever you go.

(Proverbs 3.5–6, TPT)

pages of Scripture: almost every character in the Bible was asked to do the same by God. Just think of Daniel in the lions' den when he had been loyal to God (Daniel 6), or the apostles imprisoned for sharing the good news (Acts 5), or Abraham and Sarah as they grew older in age and still had not seen the many descendants that had been promised (Genesis 17). It is the ultimate test of trust.

And what happened in the light? Daniel, the uncompromising man, went on to be elevated even higher by the king, and his enemies who had thrown him into the den were destroyed once and for all. The apostles were freed by an angel and their testimony spread further. Abraham and Sarah had a child who could only be attributed to God and his miraculous ways. God is always wanting our life stories to have him at centre stage because only then can we become a vessel that allows God's light to shine through us so that more people will see him.

God is always deepening our characters and broadening the edges of our faith so that we can walk hand in hand with him into the sustaining light of his making and not the flickering of our own. He highlights this in Isaiah 50.11 when he says:

> But watch out, you who live in your own light
>   and warm yourselves by your own fires.
> This is the reward you will receive from me:
>   You will soon fall down in great torment.

If we depend on our own talents and visions, we will develop pride, which always leads to disobedience.

OBEDIENCE

Sometimes it takes us to be afraid before we will surrender to God's ways. I've often heard testimonies of people who turned to God when they never had before because their life was at risk or they were being exposed to terrifying evil. When you go to God in such moments, he will ask you to trust him before he instructs you. Because if you do not choose to trust God in the dark, then you will not obey what he asks you to do in order to get out of it. You will trust your own logic and miss out on the extraordinary.

Some of the things God asks us to do seem ridiculous to us. Joshua was instructed to have all the Israelites march and shout loudly to bring the wall of a city down (Joshua 6). Gideon was told to reduce his army to 300 to face an army of tens of thousands (Judges 7). Moses was asked to put a stick in the sea so that the waters would part and allow the people to safely walk through (Exodus 14). Absolutely bizarre. I am sure the plans they would have crafted themselves would be very different. Perhaps Joshua would have preferred God to give them a mighty weapon that could crush a wall. And Gideon was most likely hoping God would multiply his army so that they would far outnumber their enemy. Or Moses might have dreamed God would provide a massive boat for them to safely cross the sea in. But God called them in the midst of their fear to trust him and his extraordinary plans.

Had they not been brought to that terrifying place they might have missed out on what was going to happen next by trusting God. The walls came crashing down in Jericho, Gideon and his small army defeated their vast enemy, and the sea walls parted for the Israelites. Extraordinary. There was no reasoning or logic that could explain these events. They could attribute them to nothing and no one *but* God. And that brought an everlasting *remembrance* of him, stories that are read today to remind a world gripped in fear that God moves in extraordinary ways.

If these incredible stories in the Bible aren't convincing you, here is another reference (please forgive me for this one because it is so girly and in no way biblical): Disney. When Aladdin asks Jasmine to go on a magical carpet ride, she asks whether it is safe. He replies by asking her whether she trusts him and holds out his hand to her. She is on a balcony situated pretty high off the ground, and though it's hard to judge exact measurements in a cartoon, it looks like a life-threatening jump. Despite the un-convincing assurance of her safety, she agrees to trust him, and he takes her hand and pulls her off the edge. I'm sure had she been let into the plan of a flying rug before she had seen it in action she would have opted for a night in. But if she hadn't made the jump, she would have missed the most incredible journey of her life.

DECIDING TO TRUST

First comes the decision to trust God. Trusting God waters our faith. It sustains it. Makes it grow. This faith will cause us to act on God's words more quickly the next time fear comes around and not according to the world's words of despair. We will do things his way and not our own. We will have a story to tell the world that is so incredible that God couldn't be left out of it. It wouldn't make sense without the mention of God. We will go on the most amazing journey of our lives. Hard? Absolutely. Scary? Most likely. Incredible? Most certainly. When God offers his hand to you, don't let the fear of the fall make you opt for a night in; instead, take his hand immediately and go on your magic carpet ride (I regret that cheesy line immediately).

When fear visits, it almost always returns. This is the sad truth: in our fallen world and to our broken selves, fear has a way of coming back. But these are the times when we need to remember that if God made a way for us once, he will do it again. If you are in a season of fear, look back at those altars you mentally set up or drew in your journal to remind yourself of when God met you before in a dark place and brought you into his light. Remembering is important, not only so that you can share your story and minister to others about God, enriching their lives in the process, but also because God needs you to remember him in your past so that you invite him urgently into your present and trust him wholeheartedly for your future. You need to remember so that you disregard fear and obey him more quickly.

STEP OUT OF THE BOAT

When it comes to biblical examples of ordinary people trusting an extraordinary God, I absolutely love the account of Peter walking on the water.

Peter is probably the disciple I relate to the most. He was so passionate, and that caused him to promise big and deliver small (for example, the denial at the cross in John 13.37–38; 18.15–26). Peter wasn't invited by Jesus on to the sea, so he invited Jesus to invite him to partake in the miracle (Matthew 14.22–33). Who does that? He was so in love with and passionate for Jesus and yet so infinitely human. Jesus took his hand and said, 'Why did you doubt?' and I always imagine him saying it with the kindest smile on his face, demonstrating such love and favour for 'big personality' Peter.

But here is why I respect Peter immensely. First, he *asks* Jesus to invite him into the deep end, and second, he *waits* until he does. He doesn't act until he has Christ's instruction to do so. How often we run on ahead with our dreams, and then, when we find ourselves in the deep waves, we wonder why God led us here. Pray diligently over your dreams. Ask God to call you out and then wait for the door to open, or pray for peace for a step you are about to take.

'Lord, if it's you,' Peter replied, 'tell me to come to you on the water.'

'Come,' he said.

Then Peter got down out of the boat, walked on the water and came towards Jesus. But when he saw the wind, he was afraid and, beginning to sink, cried out, 'Lord, save me!'

Immediately Jesus reached out his hand and caught him. 'You of little faith,' he said, 'why did you doubt?'

And when they climbed into the boat, the wind died down. Then those who were in the boat worshipped him, saying, 'Truly you are the Son of God.'

(Matthew 14.28–33, NIV)

Third, Peter got out of the boat! They were in the middle of a storm. And yes, we know that he took his eyes off Jesus and started to sink. But he still got out of the boat despite the winds of fear that blew all around them. He was courageous! If you are like 'big personality' Peter and you have that courage and passion within you, then you have been equipped with the braveness to step out of the boat. Just don't let your passion overtake you in a moment so that you forget to 'remain in the vine' and to keep trusting God when walking on the water. Keep your eyes on Jesus.

These moments of choosing to trust and to step out on to the water cause our faith to grow. One of these moments for me was undoubtedly choosing to pursue a music career in the secular industry. As much as God encouraged me that the well-meaning naysayers at church were wrong, it didn't get rid of all of my doubts when stepping out of the boat. Although God didn't banish my fear completely, he did promise to be with me in it. And it was during this time that I remembered again the piece of Scripture that God had written on my heart: 'I am sending you out as sheep among wolves. So be as shrewd as snakes and harmless as doves' (Matthew 10.16).

God doesn't want us to fight fear as the world does. He wants us to kneel, pray and wait on him; to walk with integrity and love for our enemies and to know that wherever we go, God goes before us.

I took that verse and wrote a song that would later become my first release as an independent artist, a song that has been playlisted on both massive worship and R&B playlists and is still my biggest independent single release to date. I wrote it as a prayer to my God, on my knees within my season of fear, reminding myself of the God who hides me under his wing and wrote his words on my heart: 'He will cover you with his feathers. He will shelter you with his wings. His faithful promises are your armor and protection' (Psalm 91.4). The God who goes before me and surrounds me. The God who calls me his child and fights my battles. Every time I perform this song, I sing it physically on my knees to remind myself of the spiritual position I took of surrendering the fight to God. And every time I perform it, I tell the audience of the way God brought me.

Wolf den

You send me out,
Walking through the forest of doubt.
I know they hear me now.
Through the moonlit trees I need your cloak to cover me.

Like a child I've wandered into the den,
Facing the foolish of the wisest men.

But I'll keep singing that sweet faith.
I'll keep singing that sweet faith.

The wolves are at my side but I know their teeth can't bite.

So I won't hide, no.

I'll keep singing that sweet faith.

You sent me on a quest

And you hid your treasure in my chest.

Maybe they don't know it yet,

That my weary eyes disguise the strength inside of me.

I won't run away, no.

I won't run away, no.

When the wolves say, 'Go home, go home,'

I'll wait for you.

It's time to let love rule my mind.

So when the wolves say, 'Go home, go home,'

I'll dare to stay right here and silence fear in the darkness.

I'll keep singing that sweet faith.

Fear is not from God. He calls us into the deep end, but as long as we keep 'singing that sweet faith' and only leave the den when he calls us to, not when we are asked to by the enemy, then we will live courageously on hope and not fear. As long as we keep our eyes on Jesus and know the **love** that he has for us – a love that casts out *all* fear (1 John 4.18) – and don't pay attention to the howls of the wolves or the wind stirring up the waves that we walk on, then we will keep stepping out of boats, singing sweet faith in the dark and walking on water.

The LORD will comfort Israel
    again
  and have pity on her ruins.
Her desert will blossom like
    Eden,
  her barren wilderness like the
    garden of the LORD.
Joy and gladness will be found
    there.
  Songs of thanksgiving will fill
    the air.

(Isaiah 51.3)

Chapter five

TRUSTING IN THE DESERT

Ever wonder why Satan chose the desert to tempt Jesus? Why not a big city that surely would have had lots more opportunities for distraction and temptation, with seductive faces, places to hide, flashy eye-catching scenery, business, drugs and getting drunk in 'da club'? (Although I'm not too sure how enticing 'da club' scene would have been in biblical times. I'm thinking more two-step sandal vibing to harps and less bump and grinding to 'apple bottom jeans'.) Nevertheless, Satan didn't choose to tempt Jesus there. He approached him in the desert. The lonely, desolate, boring-shades-of-brown, empty desert.

There is barely any life in a desert. No green shoots hinting at a blooming, fruitful season on its way. No lake of glistening water to rinse off the dirt and sand that has been stuck in the cuts on your feet. No refreshment. Just the heat of the sun making you sweat as you stare at your derelict, dry surroundings. Zero opportunities. Nothing to distract you from the pure hopelessness all around you.

The desert creates a prime setting for doubting that God has a plan. Doubting God's plan for you creates a craving for distraction via temptation. Giving in to temptation leads to shame. Shame can lead to hopelessness. And hopelessness very often leads to feeling lost and no longer trusting God with your life. Have you ever felt as though you're in that place? Do you perhaps feel you are in a desert place now?

Things started well in the aftermath of *The Voice*. However, it didn't take long before I found myself in meetings with people who wanted me to hand myself completely into their control, before I was eventually dropped from my label and my record deal. After I had been dropped, I felt as though my dreams had fallen so far from my fingertips that they were no longer tangible. I would describe myself as entering my own desert place.

Sometimes it's easy to forget how hard the desert place feels when we are no longer in it, so, in order to write this chapter, I read through old emails that I had been blind copied into, emails that no one (bar the one person who thought I should) ever wanted me to read. What these people said about me, the same people who had once told me I was the best talent to ever come their way, was devastating. These were the same people who told me to stay close to them because they had my best interests at heart. They threw me into the fire and blamed me for the flames. I became their scapegoat. I had been told constantly through the recording process that I had no power to make decisions, yet now it was my fault that the wrong ones had been made. I was described as 'finished', my 'career over'. The injustice of it all. When reading over these emails, I could remember exactly how it felt at that time.

Lonely. Unprotected. Helpless. Heartbroken. Cheated. Ruined. I saw what I thought was my whole purpose in life dry up before my eyes, and there was barely even a green bud left of any of my dreams. Just brown, dry, lifeless sand. I was desperate for a distraction, because facing the rubble of my ruins was far worse. I wanted to be busy, busy being creative and doing what I thought I was born for. But I had no funds and was tied into contracts that meant the people who had hurt me would still own what I made, despite no investment from them. I felt completely trapped. I couldn't see anything on my horizon, just a hot haze of nothingness.

I gave in to many temptations in the hope of distraction from the pain of loss, but they made me feel lost. And ashamed. I grieved everything, including the loss of my sister all over again. I felt anger at God. I felt doubt. Had God really led me into all of this? Was I a fool for thinking he was directing my path? Was I an idiot for standing up for my faith when I was asked to sing lyrics that I didn't feel honoured him? After all, now I was being told I was 'too hard to work with'. Did God even exist?

I felt empty. I felt bored. I was too scared to go out of my flat because I would be recognized, and those people would ask me what had happened to my career. And that pain and embarrassment was worse than sitting in my bedroom alone. So I would do just that every day. Honestly, when I picture that bedroom in London, all I can see in my mind is a big desert. And oh my, did the devil meet me there . . .

LOOK, WHO'S TALKING?

Very quickly, those feelings led to negative internal thinking. I gave space to what I would now call my darkest thoughts. That I was worthless. Perhaps I was no longer needed by God. Or God had chosen not to use me because I was weak. That I had been abandoned by God. That I was never intended to be on this earth and my being here was a mistake. That everyone was laughing at me. That I was a failure. That I was unwanted. That I was too beaten up to get up ever again. That I was ugly, and that is why I didn't make it as a pop star.

Have you ever wondered why when you think good and uplifting things about yourself you know the Holy Spirit is speaking, and yet when you start thinking the worst thoughts about yourself you believe it's just you talking? Why do we take Satan out of the equation? Satan is very good at voices. He's very good at sounding like *you*. When you are beating yourself up, it is the very voice and language of Satan. And it is *lies*. Let us be quicker at identifying that.

After all, Christ called Satan 'a liar and the father of lies' (John 8.44).

I don't know whether you've ever been in this place. It may be that you're there now. If you are, then I would encourage you to speak to someone who you know loves you. When my best friend struggled with thinking badly about herself, I would sit on her bed and refuse to leave, because if I did there would be no one to stick up for my friend. Telling someone we trust what we are thinking about ourselves can level the playing field. **You** against **you** when **you** are feeling low about **you** is a battle you will struggle to win. And it is a vicious circle the devil enjoys spinning. Once you invite a person in, it can stop the endless hate cycle and allow some love in.

I would also encourage you to open the door to let some light into your mind when it feels as if it is drowning in the dark. In other words, read Scripture and see what God is saying about you to drown out the devil's voice.

At that time, I needed to hear life-giving words. And so I opened my Bible. I read over the Scriptures:

What is the price of two sparrows – one copper coin? But not a single sparrow can fall to the ground without your Father knowing it. And the very hairs on your head are all numbered. So don't be afraid; you are more valuable to God than a whole flock of sparrows.

(Matthew 10.29–31)

Because you are precious in my eyes,
    and honoured, and I love you,
I give men in return for you,
    peoples in exchange for your life.

(Isaiah 43.4, ESV UK)

You watched me as I was being formed in utter seclusion,
    as I was woven together in the dark of the womb.
You saw me before I was born.
    Every day of my life was recorded in your book.
Every moment was laid out
    before a single day had passed.
How precious are your thoughts about me, O God.
    They cannot be numbered!

(Psalm 139.15–17)

I still had 'down days' but I praised, prayed, thanked and repeated these scriptures aloud and responded with poetry (which makes me sound like an intense weirdo) to creatively express the place I was in and to set up an altar to how God was meeting me and revealing his character towards me. This poetry I still read today to encourage me when I need it. I based the following on the imagery of Jonah being swallowed by the fish, and what a dark, hopeless, lonely place he must have found himself in.

In the belly of the fish

But within the belly of the fish
I call out from the depth of my pain, 'O Lord come and rescue
    me.'
And when my cry is unanswered and echoes through dark waters,
I hear the enemy, 'Little orphan, he has deserted thee.'

Get away from me, Satan.
I have no place for your lies in my heart nor my mind,
For they are full and engraved with the word of the Lord
And enable faith even though I walk blind.

Although at times I do not feel,
I find strength in what I know.
My God is the creator of all things,
And his gaze never left the falling sparrow.

How much more am I worth to him than this bird?
Even when I dwell in deep waters and my spirit is low,
How much more is his sight set firmly on me?
I am his special treasure. For the Bible told me so.

That's just it, isn't it? We need to first identify Satan as the speaker in times of dark thinking and then go to the word to see what God has to say about us. We need to be a generation that is full to the brim with Scripture so that there is literally no room for the enemy's lies in our minds and hearts. I remember reading a Joyce Meyer book called *Battlefield of the Mind* where she portrays this in an image that has always stayed with me. She describes a man who has demons clinging to his head and whispering lies into his ears. The man opens his mouth and starts to speak Scripture aloud. Every time he opens his mouth to speak the words of God, swords of light come out of it and the demons flee. As Hebrews 4.12 tells us, 'For the word of God is alive and powerful. It is sharper than the sharpest two-edged sword, cutting between soul and spirit, between joint and marrow.'

This is exactly what Jesus did in the desert place when the devil was tempting him.

So when Satan makes you think, 'I am ugly, worthless. Not meant to be here,' say, 'No! The Scriptures say, "I am fearfully and wonderfully made"' (Psalm 139.14, NIV).

When Satan causes you to think, 'I am trapped. Grounded by chains,' say, 'No! The Scriptures say, "Wherever the Spirit of the Lord is, there is freedom"' (2 Corinthians 3.17).

During that time the devil came and said to him, 'If you are the Son of God, tell these stones to become loaves of bread.'

But Jesus told him, 'No! The Scriptures say,

"People do not live by bread alone,

but by every word that comes from the mouth of God."'

(Matthew 4.3–4)

When Satan makes you think, 'I am alone,' say, 'No! The Scriptures say, "For the LORD your God will personally go ahead of you. He will neither fail you nor abandon you"' (Deuteronomy 31.6).

START TO PRAISE

Lift your spirit by speaking the language of God. He doesn't need our praise to feel good about himself. We need to praise him to feel good about ourselves. It is what we are designed for: 'The people I formed for myself that they may proclaim my praise' (Isaiah 43.21, NIV).

I remember asking my mum, who had lost her marriage and her firstborn daughter, how she ever found things to praise God for. She said she would start small: 'Thank you, God, for how beautiful the sky looks today.' Once she had started thanking God for the small things, she said, her heart would begin to leap for joy and before she knew it she couldn't stop praising him for all the joys in her life. She didn't need to wait for something 'big'; she just needed to begin.

Start right now. Begin. As the psalmist says, 'I lift up my eyes to the mountains – where does my help come from? My help comes from the LORD, the Maker of heaven and earth' (Psalm 121.1–2, NIV). Lift your eyes up from your situation and begin to praise your creator who loves you more than you can imagine. Praising God starts to clear the mist. You start to have a change of perspective – a more heavenly one. Not one where you completely abandon the hurt of the past, but one where you see there is a road ahead of you. You will not be in the desert for ever.

CHANGING PERSPECTIVE

Have you read *God on Mute* by Pete Greig? If anything I've written resonates with you, please read it. And if nothing I have written resonates with you, then please read it anyway. There are so many insights to gain from his raw honesty about his journey through pain and delayed instruction or answer from God. At a time when I couldn't make sense of why God had equipped me with a voice and passion for people in the industry and yet was holding me back from being in it, the truths I learnt from this book stood out to me.

Pete draws on a story of a king who had three sons who were all due their inheritance. With his favourite son, he delayed giving the inheritance to him. His reasoning was not torture, but rather he knew that once he had given it, his son would leave with it. And he wanted to keep him in his courts, to spend more time with him. How often we forget that God desires to talk with us, to have fellowship with us. And how much more often do we spend time with God when we are so in need or desire something. It isn't a selfish act from God; our spending time with him is the source of life.

If only we could learn to remain in God's courts, to remain in the vine, through all our seasons. But for now, if you are in your desert place, on your knees before the one true God, take comfort in the fact that not only does he hear you and hasn't forgotten you, but he is also loving spending time with you. Remembering Pete's words changed my perspective of what God was doing with me in this time, and I wrote this:

For such a time as this

For such a time as this
I have been brought to my knees to pray,
To be silent and seek his word,
For there is no light guiding my way.

I will not fill my life with pointless activities
That bring no meaning to the end.
I will quiet my soul and silence my worry
And sit in the counsel of my Lord, my friend.

Though he has closed all the doors
And has hidden his path from my sight,
Locking me in his presence
To teach me that I am his delight.

In Exodus 15 we see that the Israelites needed a change of perspective. Right after they had been rescued from Egypt, freed from years of slavery, when God had performed a mighty miracle of splitting the sea so they could pass through safely on dry land, the chapter doesn't end before they began to moan about the desert place they found themselves in. It had been three days and they hadn't found drinkable water or any food to eat. As much as I would love to believe I would have praised instead of moaned, I'm pretty confident my reaction to this situation would have been as human as theirs was (considering that on our honeymoon we got lost on a very remote beach and couldn't find water in the 38-degree heat for three hours and my only reaction was to bawl my eyes out like a two-year-old).

What was God's response to their moaning? He provided manna from heaven and water from a rock. He *provided* for them despite their grumbles. You may think to yourself that this was strange – surely he should have taught them a good lesson first. He did teach them lessons of obedience and faithfulness, but he provided for their needs *first*. Please remember he was their parent. He is also *your* perfect heavenly parent!

When my son has a tantrum because he has handed me the biscuit tin while I'm preparing his dinner for him, I don't throw his food in the bin and leave him screaming hungry. I put the tin back in the cupboard and lift my hungry boy into his high chair to feed him his dinner. He is my son and I want him to live, so I'm going to provide for his basic needs, no matter what! Perhaps if the Israelites had understood that God was their Father and his love for them as his children was too great to leave them to die, maybe they could have enjoyed praising and trusting him to provide for them. If only I had understood that sooner too . . .

When I began to thank God for the things in my life, starting small, it opened my eyes to the fact God had provided for me. I have always been blessed by creative and talented people around me who have been so generous with their time and gifts when I can afford to pay them nothing. Without them I would be incapable of keeping my music going, which thankfully I still enjoy making to this day. During my time in London, every month I would receive income from something or other. My heavenly Father was providing for my basic needs, *despite* my moaning and *before* he taught me some life-saving lessons. It was at this time that I decided to read the book of Isaiah.

Written by the prophet Isaiah, the first 39 chapters are a call to the nations of Judah and Israel and to the surrounding nations to repent of their sins and come back to God. The last 27 chapters are filled with hope and comfort as Isaiah proclaims God's promise of an incredible future through the coming of Jesus.

As I read through Isaiah, my spirit leapt. I wept. And I fell to my knees before God. God always plans to rebuild our ruins. He is the creator, not the destroyer, and he gives us this life-giving promise among the barren rubble. To restore. To renew. To rejoice. God is always working in the new. Beth Moore, in her book *Breaking Free*, reminds us that God is always described

I am the LORD, who opened a way
        through the waters,
    making a dry path through the sea . . .
But forget all that –
    it is nothing compared to what I am
        going to do.
For I am about to do something new.
    See, I have already begun! Do you not
        see it?
(Isaiah 43.16, 18–19)

The LORD will comfort Israel again
    and have pity on her ruins.
Her desert will blossom like Eden,
    her barren wilderness like the garden
        of the LORD.
Joy and gladness will be found there.
    Songs of thanksgiving will fill the air.
(Isaiah 51.3)

as being on the move. He is a 'river' or a 'bubbling brook' or a 'fountain'. He is never described as a stagnant pond. He, of course, meets us to comfort our souls as we mourn the past, but he wants us to know that he has already begun to work on our future.

HOPE IN THE SAND

I don't know about you, but I've been to too many Christian youth events where the well-known poem 'Footprints in the Sand' has been presented in a cringy PowerPoint presentation full of floaty white linen and bare feet. Now I almost feel that the beautiful point of it has been lost deep down in my cynicism. But there **is** a beautiful point to be made in this poem, which is probably why it is used so often. And the point is simple: God is with you.

Perhaps you have to be in a hard, dull place to see the evidence of God carrying you, walking in front of you and beside you. You can't see footprints on a beautiful day walking on the spongy grass. But you can see them clearly in the sticky mud or sandy desert. Perhaps God saved you from something, or perhaps he just allowed it for some heavenly reason you can't fathom with your earthly mind. But he didn't just leave you to it. He walked you through it. If you could look back on that dark place in your life, whether you knew it and felt it or not, you were walking under the wing of your creator. As the psalmist in Psalm 91.4 (NIV) puts it, 'He will cover you with his feathers, and under his wings you will find refuge.'

It may not feel like it now, but the Bible assures us that God has plans to make your desert, your barren land, blossom more than the garden of Eden. I hope, like it does for me, this helps you start to trust the plans God has for you. Trust him to rebuild you on your ruins. To give you hope.

If you're struggling to put your trust in him, begin to praise him. Start small and soon you will see the joys he has in store for you. Perhaps one day we will be so joyful that we can even enjoy PowerPoint presentations of white linen again. (Most likely not, though.)

'For I know the plans I have for you,' declares the LORD, 'plans to prosper you and not to harm you, plans to give you hope and a future.'

(Jeremiah 29.11, NIV)

Chapter six
PLANS NOT TO HARM YOU

'I know the plans I have for you . . . plans to prosper you and not to harm you.' If you've been around church for any length of time, you've probably heard this beautiful scripture repeated time and time again. I see this verse quoted a lot by celebrities, or written on the bio of Instagram accounts of celebrities from whom I have never heard any other declaration of faith. Perhaps it is a verse that suits us as a society, one that is driven by the sentiment, 'You can be whatever and whoever you want to be.' The idea that there is a supernatural power working behind the scenes to make all our dreams come true and drive us to greatness while protecting us from all heartache is very attractive. But when we are faced with the reality that the blueprints we have drawn for our own lives are very often not the sketches God is working from, we crumble.

And it's not just celebrities who want to capture and celebrate this sticky-note-style scripture; many of us were taught to trust this verse very early on in our walk with Jesus. This was the verse that was given to me by my dad at my baptism when I was 14 years old. It became the verse I carried around in my pocket for the next decade, only to then become the verse I struggled with the most.

I think I had a fundamental flaw in my understanding of God and his plans. I believed that, because I loved God, he was going to make all my dreams come true and nothing terribly bad would happen to me. It's not that I didn't believe storms would come; it is just that I believed I would sail through life without being shipwrecked because God had these prosperous plans for me. But I have been shipwrecked many times and I have felt harmed and wounded beyond repair. And it was in these times that I started to lose trust in God and his plans and promises. But were they ever *his* plans and promises to begin with?

GOD'S PLANS, NOT MINE

I think this verse is a great example of how we should not pick out scriptures that suit our own agenda and then take a black marker pen to the bits that don't. How many times do we highlight a verse in the Bible and then close the pages instead of reading the Scripture around it?

This very verse was written to the Israelites who were in exile because they had disobeyed God. They were already experiencing a season of harm, of which they themselves had been the makers. The Israelites wanted a quick escape from their suffering, but instead God told them they were going to stay there and help the nation to which they were slaves flourish. He *was* going to rescue them, but it would be their great-grandchildren in 70 years' time who would be delivered home, and not them. They wanted a quick fix, but God had different plans.

The verses straight after verse 11 that are rarely quoted require a heart shift from looking for a miracle act from God to ourselves: 'In those days when you pray, I will listen. If you look for me wholeheartedly, you will find me.' The Israelites needed to put God first, to earnestly pray and seek after God with all of their being. How often do we forget the verses that either require something from us or remind us that God's plans for us are very often not the same as our own? This is heightened in Isaiah 55.8–9:

'My thoughts are nothing like your thoughts,'
     says the LORD.
  'And my ways are far beyond anything you
       could imagine.
For just as the heavens are higher than the
     earth,
  so my ways are higher than your ways
  and my thoughts higher than your thoughts.'

Very often we read the Bible with our own situations in mind. Had I forgotten that the entire earth was created by God speaking it into formation and therefore he is better at designing my future than I am? And that my life is part of a far more intricate design, woven together along with the lives of many others to glorify God? If he created the whole world, he definitely sees a much bigger and more exciting picture than I do. We have to continually align ourselves with his heart and check that we are working towards glorifying him and pointing people to Jesus and not to ourselves. Jesus heightened this when he said:

> I tell you the truth, anyone who believes in me will do the same works I have done, and even greater works, because I am going to be with the Father. You can ask for anything in my name, and I will do it, so that the Son can bring glory to the Father. Yes, ask me for anything in my name, and I will do it!
>
> (John 14.12–14)

In the same way that we can hold on to Jeremiah 29.11 as evidence that God will see our dreams come to pass, Jesus' words in John 14.12–14 are also often misinterpreted as God being a giant blue genie. But, honestly, if every person's wishes were granted, think of the mayhem our world would go into. Every evil thing in this world starts with a selfish desire. And we are human and can't help but have such desires. At the start of this verse, Jesus says, 'Anyone who believes in me will do the same works I have done.' His work was as incredibly selfless as he was. A heart that is doing the same work as Christ, that desires to see God glorified and is so in tune with the Father, will ask for things in Jesus' name and they will be granted. God will not grant something that is not according to his will.

Our expectations of God and what we think he is going to do for us are often not aligned with his plans for us. And so we feel let down when he doesn't read from the script we have written for our own lives. But I believe God's plans for us are bigger than we are and are worth seeking instead of our own. Don't get me wrong, though – I do believe a lot of our dreams are firmly established in us because God put them there.

When I was a teenager, I was about to do the biggest gig I had done so far. It was in front of around 3,000 people and I was suitably nervous – to the point where I was wondering, 'Why do I even do this to myself?' I prayed to God to please take my nerves away, but he never did, and as it got closer and closer to the gig, they were getting worse. I prayed again, 'Lord, please won't you take my nerves away?'

I felt him say to me, 'My child, go and delight in the gifts I have given you, like I delight in seeing you use them.' These are now the words I hear spoken over me before every performance, whether to an audience of 100 or in front of 20,000.

God loves seeing us use the gifts he has given us. It might not always be on a platform the world would value or deem successful, but even to an audience of one the show is still beautiful. He wants us not only to use those gifts but also to remember to *enjoy* them! Have you ever put so much pressure on yourself that you forgot the childlike joy of doing something that came naturally to you that you previously loved doing? Drama, writing, sport, playing an instrument: whatever it is, just enjoying doing that thing without the pressure of becoming the best, the most famous or being able to pay bills with it is pleasing to God.

God never did take my nerves away. In fact, when I was singing on *The Voice* in front of millions of people they got significantly worse. But my nerves reminded me to invite God into that moment, and before every performance I heard him saying those words, reminding me that he wanted me to delight in my gifts. Soon I found my focus turn from the crowds and the cameras to my audience of one and I remembered whom I was singing for. My God, who is not judgemental or waiting for me to fail or going to snigger if I burp during a song (happened), or if my sweaty palms make the microphone slip out of my hand (also happened), is a proud Father in heaven who delights in seeing me use the voice he designed and gave me. I am glad taking away my nerves was not according to his will; they keep me kneeling to God before every performance.

His plans for you are very likely not going to be exactly what you thought you wanted. He is a good God and therefore his plans for you will involve you using your gifts. His plans can be trusted wholeheartedly because they are higher than your own. They are for the greater good. They are the best plans for the many others he wants you to help. They are to give you hope and to keep pushing you forward into your future. They are for glorifying Jesus and for bringing meaning and purpose to your life by worshipping him with your whole being.

WILL WE NOW BE HARM FREE?

But the question still remains: are his plans for us absent of *all* harm? From looking at all the characters in the Bible, I don't believe they are. Daniel sat in a den overnight with lions (Daniel 6); Joseph, though innocent, spent many years in jail (Genesis 39–41); Moses walked for 40 years in the desert (the books of Exodus, Leviticus, Numbers and Deuteronomy); Paul was shipwrecked (Acts 27.27–44); Job lost everything before he gained (book of Job); and Jesus was crucified (Matthew 27.32–56).

We have already seen that when Jeremiah prophesied, the Israelites were in exile, *in* a season of harm. But God had plans to bring good *out* of it. God has an incredible future for us in heaven, but on earth we will experience suffering. Even James wrote:

> Consider it pure joy, my brothers and sisters, whenever you
> face trials of many kinds, because you know that the testing

of your faith produces perseverance. Let perseverance finish
its work so that you may be mature and complete, not
lacking anything.

(James 1.2–4, NIV)

You will face times of feeling shipwrecked, at the end of yourself.
May you trust God that it will pass, and may you learn how to
flourish in the midst of it.

DID GOD *CAUSE* ME HARM?

Jeremiah 29.11 does not say 'free of <u>*all* harm</u>', but it's easy for our
trust to falter when we start to wonder whether God has *caused*
us harm. Did he cause my sister to have an accident? Did he set
me up to be so close to fulfilling my music dreams so that I
would fall harder? The question of whether or not God knowing
something is going to happen and not stopping it counts as him
causing us harm is enough to make my head hurt. And yet, in my
heart, I know that my God does not set me up to hurt me.

I love reading the Bible and am always looking to know more
about my heavenly Father, yet I have a childlike faith in many
ways, and I think that is sometimes necessary. It's also something
that Jesus encourages in his followers:

[Jesus] called a little child to him and put the child among
them. Then he said, 'I tell you the truth, unless you turn
from your sins and become like little children, you will

never get into the Kingdom of Heaven. So anyone who becomes as humble as this little child is the greatest in the Kingdom of Heaven.'
(Matthew 18.2–4)

At these times of questioning whether God would set me up for my falls, I lean on this childlike faith. That is not my God. That is not the God of the Bible. He is the God of mercy and kindness. The God of justice, yes, but the God who saw the biggest debt in exchange for justice that needed to be paid by humanity and paid it himself. The God of incomprehensible love, forgiveness and patience for his people. When we read the Old Testament we see a God so fiercely protective of his people. Would that God *cause* harm to come to you?

All good things are formed by him and are from him. We aren't in heaven yet; we live in a fallen world that is full of the consequences of sin and ultimately death because we chose ourselves over him and his ways. However, as we read in Romans 8.28, 'God causes everything to work together for the good of those who love God and are called according to his purpose for them.' And he never, ever leaves us alone in it.

BUT HE CAN PROTECT US FROM HARM, SO WHY DOESN'T HE?

Honestly, I don't know. There are some things I think we just won't fully understand until we get to heaven and are of perfect

Don't be deceived, my dear brothers and sisters. Every good and perfect gift is from above, coming down from the Father of the heavenly lights, who does not change like shifting shadows. He chose to give us birth through the word of truth, that we would be a kind of firstfruits of all he created.

(James 1.16–18, NIV)

thinking. For example, if God were to tell me now that he allowed the accident that led to my sister's death to happen because at my sister's funeral three people would come to know Jesus, admittedly and with shame I would say it wasn't a good enough reason. You might be shocked by that. Or you too might have a pain in your life that you feel there is no reason big enough that would justify it. Perhaps here on earth we are not yet equipped to understand God's reasons, but when I get to heaven and meet those three people who will now spend eternity with their saviour because of the way we praised Jesus in Rebekah's death, maybe I'll fully understand. Maybe, in light of their eternal lives (and being united with my sister once again), I may even be grateful for her accident. Maybe, when I get to heaven, I will be so full of supernatural understanding that I won't even need to ask why! After all, the Scriptures do say, 'For now we see only a reflection as in a mirror; then we shall see face to face. Now I know in part; then I shall know fully, even as I am fully known' (1 Corinthians 13.12, NIV).

But for now, I know God is patient with me and meets me in my anger, my humanity and my lack of understanding. He weeps with me, holds my hand and leads me through this world with him. And we know that God uses the heartbroken to speak to the heartbroken. I don't know about you, but when I listen to preachers speak, I feel that their words carry much more weight when they share painful stories about their own lives. It shows that they've been there, that they may understand a small part of what I'm going through.

We need to experience heartbreak to reach more people, because the world is broken. Yes, the characters I previously mentioned were harmed, but Daniel advised kings (Daniel 4); Joseph led a nation out of famine (Genesis 41.41–57); Moses delivered God's people from slavery to the promised land (the book of Joshua); Paul brought hundreds to Christ (the book of Acts); Job received full restoration and then some (Job 42); and Jesus paid the debt we owed, conquered death and made a way for us to have freedom from sin on earth and to live for eternity in heaven, praising him with the ones we lost who love his name (John 3.16). Amen.

I believe that, despite the fact that God does not cause these heartbreaks to happen, he allows them, to shape our characters, to deepen our trust in him and to prove his faithfulness to us along the way. We read in Psalm 105.19, 'Until the time came to fulfill his dreams, the LORD tested Joseph's character.'

In Joseph's case, the dreams were prophecies that God had given to him as a boy. You may have had things spoken over you by people with the gift of prophecy, or you may have had dreams like this yourself. Maybe you have just always had an ambition and know you have been equipped for it. I'm sure Joseph doubted those dreams had been from God when he was sitting in a jail surrounded by bars. In fact, I'm almost positive he felt like an idiot for having shared them.

Maybe that is you now. I know for sure it is me. And right now, if you feel as though you are looking at bars instead of fulfilled promises, know that God is the Father of truth. He did not lie to you. He is incapable of breaking promises and telling lies. If you remain in the vine and are trusting in him, you will become all that he wants you to be. But he cares too much about you and the people on your path to go against his perfect timing. If Joseph had been given authority and placed in a position of power before he had felt what it was like to be powerless under an authority that had abused its position, then perhaps it would not have been in his character to be so merciful to his brothers or so loving to the nation. If he had not felt what it was like to have only God in his nothing, then maybe he would not have wanted only God in his everything.

I hope you can start to trust that, because God loves you more than you can fathom, his heavenly reasons for *allowing* harm to come to you are to enrich your character and further your reach to his lost children.

PREVENTED HARM

Let us also remember that when God saves us from harm, we are not always aware of it because it never happens. It is *prevented*.

While I was in the middle of my album being shelved and the label dropping me, I heard a speaker at Hillsong London. He told a story about hearing his two-year-old daughter giggling and laughing in the distance, his favourite sound in the world. She was playing with something and he couldn't wait to go and see what it was. When he got closer to her, he saw that it was a scorpion. Fear froze him to the spot. He had two options: to gently try to explain to his daughter the danger of this scorpion with the aim of coaxing her out of this life-threatening situation, or to immediately lift her up and kill the creature. As a father, he chose the second option without a moment's thought. Afterwards, did the daughter say, 'Thank you, Daddy; you saved me from that danger'? No. Her lack of ability to understand what her father had done caused her to immediately start screaming and crying because Daddy had killed her 'best friend'.

The preacher stopped at this point and addressed the congregation: 'Some of you cannot understand why God has killed something that you were so enjoying. You don't even know that he just saved you from something that was going to harm or possibly kill you.'

I cried in that moment even though I wasn't completely sure I knew why. God did kill my career in the direction it was going. I felt that there was no voice from God, no reasoning to give me a heads-up or to let me make my own decision about the situation. But looking back, I can see the toll that the ups and downs of pursuing this dream were taking on me. I met some massive celebrities during my time in LA and was able to see how the industry was also affecting their mental health and sense of self-worth. Now I look back and wonder whether I was saved from something that would have ultimately harmed me greatly or even caused me to harm myself. I will never know until I get to heaven. What I do know, however, is that every time I am in a season of despair and I put myself in a place where I can listen to God and hear him speak, he meets with me like he did in that moment to give me hope and to remind me that he loves me more than I can ever imagine. In this quiet place, he reminds me once again that he is always there, lifting me out of harmful situations so that they become my past and he can set me back down into a position where I can trust him with my future.

I hope you choose to trust that God loves you so much that he is constantly protecting you and would never allow harm to come to you without there being a heavenly reason. One day we will understand. But for now, may he draw close.

SELF-HARM

In addition to the harm we don't understand and the prevented harm we cannot see, a lot of our heartbreak is caused by abandoning God's ways and living in the consequences of sin.

This is not something I deal with well. I'm not sure about you, but I tend to reason my way out of the uncomfortableness of these consequences by saying that it's God changing my direction rather than it being his correction. Either that or I go to the other extreme and decide that because I have failed, I am a *failure*. I will not amount to anything because I have completely disobeyed God and am therefore no longer useful to him. I almost abandon my trust in God because I do not think I am trustworthy; I don't trust myself to be obedient.

My point is, be careful that you do not get so caught up in assigning blame to God or to yourself that you lose the gold of a lesson of grace to be learned, which is buried among your self-made mess. There is self-harm when we sin. That is why God does not want us to do it. It was not caused by God; it was caused by us, but because of what Christ has done for us, because of his perfect grace, God can bring good out of it. If we let him. And he goes further than that. Because Christ has dealt with your sins on the cross, the Father does not want you to feel shame for those things for which you have now asked and received forgiveness. In fact, when you go ashamed to him, he sings mercy over you.

I used to joke that I wanted to be a pop star 'for Jesus', but when things started to go well for me, the pause in the 'for Jesus' part of my dream became longer. And it wasn't because I was blinded by the lights, excitement and fast pace of it all. It was the unexpected disappointment of it all. The boredom of the waiting. I expected to love it, and when I was in LA, so close to reaching my childhood fantasies (for Jesus), I was lonelier than I ever thought possible. I waited in hotel rooms for days without seeing anyone until specific people became available to work with me. It was the stress of knowing that things were not aligning and that every day it could all be closer to slipping through my fingers. I felt God had let me be controlled by people who didn't have my best interests at heart, but, truth be told, only I had allowed that to happen. And when the inevitable day came of everything actually slipping through my fingers, I felt anger towards God, and my decisions got worse still. Needless to say, my 'distractions' resulted in me feeling more lonely, more worthless and more like a failure. And to top it all, I felt too ashamed to come to God. I felt angry at God for my dreams falling down dead, but it was I who had decided to create a mess in the wake.

In the first chapter of Isaiah, God was dealing with his people who had forgotten him. They kept up the formalities of religion while ignoring his heart for the people who needed help. They had introduced pagan ways of worship and idolatry yet tried to mask them as for the Lord. The scripture says:

Why do you continue to invite
    punishment?
  Must you rebel forever?
Your head is injured
    and your heart is sick.

You are battered from head to foot –
  covered with bruises, welts and infected
      wounds –
  without any soothing ointments or bandages.
(Isaiah 1.5–6)

The emotive language used here sounds to me like a father's heart breaking for his lost children. He was angry at their sins and their rebellion against him. They chose to be seduced by evil, and because God is perfect he could not lavish the blessing and healing he had for them like he wanted to because he could not dwell there. But he took no satisfaction in his children having to suffer in it even though they had chosen to. His people were not looking at him or for him, their thoughts did not even include him, and yet in the middle of this chapter sits the verse of redemption in Isaiah 1.18 that we sing across the world today in many hymns:

Though your sins are like scarlet,
  I will make them as white as snow.
Though they are red like crimson,
  I will make them as white as wool.

No matter what situation you are in, or what trouble you might have got yourself into, please know that God has a redemption plan. Just as his help is the reason for your success, his forgiveness is sufficient for your failure. He longs first to soothe you and then to heal your wounds. He desires to bring you out of the mud you feel stuck in and to put your feet firmly on a rock. But he needs to get close enough to you to do that. Will you let him?

We need to stop giving in to distractions and instead turn our attention to God. Allow your heart to hear the song of Jesus, the melodies of mercies that mend the brokenness. Do not let the enemy lie to you to make you feel you have gone too far and that God cannot reach you there. God sent his Son to die for us! Do not waste time trying to assign blame or feeling shame or punishing yourself. Make this change of direction a time for God's correction. Allow him to put you on a path that is not of your own making but has been carved out by the carpenter who loves you so much he died for you. And enjoy the endless grace he cannot wait to lavish on you.

> But don't, dear friend, resent GOD's discipline;
>> don't sulk under his loving correction.
> It's the child he loves that GOD corrects;
>> a father's delight is behind all this.
> (Proverbs 3.11–12, *The Message*)

Then, when you are ready, ask God to give you new dreams. Dreams that have not been tainted by self-desire or self-harm. Dreams that will make you a vessel so that others can be soothed and healed by the Spirit of the Lord that flows through you.

Remember that ultimately all of God's plans for us have the centre focus of glorifying him by helping those with needs. Oh my, what a purpose you are going to have!

For you are a holy people, who belong to the LORD your God. Of all the people on earth, the LORD your God has chosen you to be his own special treasure.

(Deuteronomy 7.6)

Chapter seven

TRUSTING YOUR IDENTITY

I'm Northern Irish. As a people we are so friendly that personal space is often highly violated. You will be hugged. You will be spoken to on public transport whether you hide behind your book or not. You will hear our stories even if we told you them last week. Our strength and our weakness is that our humour is sarcastic and entirely self-deprecating. We will rarely tell you a story where we come off well, because that would be 'cocky' to us and not funny. It literally makes my whole body cringe to start speaking out positive things about myself. But what we say has an impact on what we think, and when you can't speak positive things out about yourself it probably means you aren't thinking positive things about yourself either.

The root meaning of the word 'trust' in the fourteenth century was described as 'confident expectation'. Scripture tells us in Jeremiah 17.7 (NIV), 'But blessed is the one who trusts in the LORD, whose confidence is in him.' If we can be confident in who God says he is, then we can learn to be confident in who God says we are.

IDENTITY

In my darkest moment, after my label had dropped me and contractually I wasn't able to release music, I felt like a ghost. I felt I had lost who I was and my purpose if I couldn't sing. Before this, whenever I introduced myself I would always say, 'Hi, I'm Leah. I'm a singer.' I had never realized how much of who I was was wrapped up in what I did until I wasn't doing it any more. Being a singer had become my entire identity.

A conversation with someone new is always, 'Hi, such and such. I'm such and such,' followed by a series of get-to-know-you questions that usually starts with, 'So what do you do?' It quickly became my most dreaded question. What was I going to say now?

Do you ever find yourself reading the Gospel of John and stalling at the sentence that is talking about John himself, where it reads, 'the disciple Jesus loved' (John 13.23). Is John not the author of this Gospel? How annoying is John? Why is he pausing after writing his own name to tell us how favoured, loved and treasured he was by Jesus? How arrogant. How infuriatingly confident. How cocky. How . . . *wise*.

John was so secure in how much Jesus loved him. And rather than measuring his worth by how faithful and good *he was* to God, he measured his worth by how much Jesus was faithful and good *to him*. This kept him so rooted and steadfast that he was the only disciple who stayed by Jesus' feet and didn't flee when they arrested and crucified him. He writes 'the disciple Jesus loved' as though it is his second name. I wonder what would happen if we were to write our names like that. 'Leah the-one-Jesus-loves McFall.' Could we be so deeply rooted in God's love for us that no matter what storm we face in life we never question our identity? We would never be tempted to give in to distractions that would lead us to unknowingly bow to another. We, like John, would, until the end, always be found faithfully at Jesus' feet.

Mary Magdalene knew of God's love for her and so was found at Jesus' feet many times. If she had focused on the labels of shame that had been spoken over her – and no doubt she had also spoken them over herself many times – then she would have been found in a dark corner somewhere, hiding from Jesus. But knowing our identity is rooted in the love *God has for us* – and not in ours for him, which is always fleeting, imperfect and human – will leave us with an unshakable identity in Christ.

Write your name out like that now and stare at it. _____
the-one-Jesus-loves _____. That is who you are. No matter what label of negativity has been spoken over you by

either yourself or someone else. You are the one Jesus loves! So much so that he died so he could spend eternity with you! No other label is the truth.

CHILD OF GOD

At times we can lose the understanding of our place in the kingdom of God. Perhaps you are so filled with the shame of your past that you don't want to accept the title 'son/daughter of the most-high King'. Or maybe you don't see yourself as worthy to be 'a friend of Jesus'. We aren't. Not even the best of us is worthy of such titles. But that is what we are called throughout Scripture, and it is not by our own merit but by Christ's that we have been given these heavenly labels by God. And since we believe all words of God to be the truth, then the titles he has bestowed on you are true, even if you struggle to believe them!

My mum often says that had King David been in church with us today, no one would want to sit beside him. He sent a faithful and good man to die on the front line of his army so he could take his wife, whom he had already slept with and made pregnant, for his own (2 Samuel 11). And yet, David was described by God as 'a man after His own heart' (1 Samuel 13.14, NKJV). Mum tells us this to teach us that God forgives in a way that humans should aspire to. The psalmist, whom many believe to be King David himself, says, 'As far as the east is from the west, so far has he removed our transgressions from us' (Psalm 103.12, NIV).

This story has assured me that God often puts titles on us that we may feel we don't deserve, but his forgiveness is complete and what he says comes to be. You are not an orphan, cast down from your place in the kingdom, no matter how much you think you have missed the mark. 'For you are all children of God through faith in Christ Jesus' (Galatians 3.26).

There are many incredible titles that God lavishes upon us but, to me, 'child of God' feels so intimate. It offers us the chance to be childlike again. To enjoy the freedom of wholly trusting a parent who is perfect and cannot break our trust. It allows us the opportunity to belong to the heavenly family, to be a part of the world church with Christ at the centre and God as the Father. My own son is going through a phase where he doesn't want to leave us at all. He just wants to be with his parents right now, and to be honest I would much rather just be with him than have to leave him to go to work. Our relationship with God as his child has no earthly restrictions like this.

I don't know what your relationship with your parents is like, but God, your perfect heavenly Father, is incapable of hurting you. You will never have to reach your arms out and cry while he drives off to work. You will never be abandoned. You will never be an orphan. **You will never be alone again.**

God is not asking us to become *childish*, but rather to humble ourselves and to have sincere and trusting hearts. I love Scripture

See how very much our Father loves us, for he calls us his children, and that is what we are! But the people who belong to this world don't recognize that we are God's children because they don't know him.

(1 John 3.1)

and seek to study it regularly, but there are times when I choose to believe God knows instead of arguing about topics that feel a bit too heavenly for my earthly brain. Having our identity so rooted in being a child of God allows us to be secure both in going deeper into our knowledge of God and in our relationship with him, and it also enables us to know when we can just be the child and let him be the parent. Being confident in the fact that I am God's child gives me the freedom to enjoy life, to play and to dream. Being a child of God makes me feel safe to love all the weird and wonderful things he has woven together inside me. What's more, asking your heavenly parent 'Why?' and 'Are we there yet?' repeatedly will *not* make him go mad! It's OK to ask God questions, so go ahead and freely ask.

SPECIAL TREASURE

While I was on *The Voice*, I was reading Deuteronomy and came across the verse where God said to the Israelites in the desert, 'For you are a holy people, who belong to the LORD your God. Of all the people on earth, the LORD your God has chosen you to be his own special treasure' (Deuteronomy 7.6). It felt as though God really wanted me to know that I belonged to him before I was put on a platform to the world. That I was his, and he *treasured* me. I soon began to understand why.

One year later, I had been sitting in meetings for months where people fought over who I belonged to, who I was legally bound to, whose bank account the profits of my God-given talent would benefit. I was always reminded of this verse as God said to my soul, 'You are my special treasure.' I wasn't a product that needed to be changed and shaped differently in order to be packaged up and presented for sale. No contract could bind me for long when I was already owned by the eternal God, the breaker of chains. This brought me and continues to bring me such comfort.

I want to encourage you to rejoice in belonging to a God who reminds you of your worth to him when others or even you yourself try to make you feel worthless. Doubting what you are worth to God can make you lack courage to step out of the boat when Jesus calls you to walk on water. Are you frightened that he would let you drown? If so, you don't know how much you are worth to him!

At the time when I felt like a ghost, when I was allowing Satan to thrive in my mind, I got on my knees and cried to God. I asked him through my tears who I was. Was I meant to be here? I felt a silence forced upon me and God saying, 'Leah, do you know I thought of you when I was on the cross? Your entire life came through my mind . . . and so I stayed there.' We can't know for sure what Christ thought about on the cross, but we do know that he went to the cross for many but would have done it for only one (Luke 15.3–7). The Scriptures tell us many times that he knew us and called us to be his own before we were even born: 'For he chose us in him before the creation of the world to be holy and blameless in his sight' (Ephesians 1.4, NIV). How

But God, being rich in mercy, because of the great love with which he loved us, even when we were dead in our trespasses, made us alive together with Christ – by grace you have been saved – and raised us up with him and seated us with him in the heavenly places in Christ Jesus, so that in the coming ages he might show the immeasurable riches of his grace in kindness towards us in Christ Jesus. For by grace you have been saved through faith. And this is not your own doing; it is the gift of God.

(Ephesians 2.4–8, ESV UK)

marvellous it is to think that before you even existed, Jesus died for you. What are you worth? To him you are worth his death.

God, who delighted in creating you and loves you more than you will ever understand, calls you his child, his special treasure, the one whom he loves. He has solidified your identity in him so that you will walk in strength in his purpose for you. Of course he has a purpose for you! Can it be trusted? Of course it can be trusted. Has he already revealed it? Yes. Where? Obviously I'm going to say in the Bible. It may not be as complex as you had thought or maybe even hoped for. But it is a purpose with the most incredible impact for the world.

PURPOSE

Thoughts about who you are and what you have been created for very often come one immediately after the other. Once God had solidified who I was in him at a time when I had lost my identity from lost dreams, my very next question was, 'What is your purpose for me, then?' We all have a yearning in us to believe we are useful. That we are wanted. That we have a reason to be on this earth. A reason to have been designed the way we are.

God once again answered my question through Scripture:

> The Lord called me before my birth;
>> from within the womb he called me by name.
> He made my words of judgment as sharp as a sword.

He has hidden me in the shadow of his hand.

I am like a sharp arrow in his quiver.

He said to me, 'You are my servant, Israel,

and you will bring me glory.'

I replied, 'But my work seems so useless!

I have spent my strength for nothing and to no purpose.

Yet I leave it all in the LORD's hand;

I will trust God for my reward.'

And now the LORD speaks –

the one who formed me in my mother's womb to be his
servant,

who commissioned me to bring Israel back to him.

The LORD has honored me,

and my God has given me strength.

He says, 'You will do more than restore the people of Israel to me.

I will make you a light to the Gentiles,

and you will bring my salvation to the ends of the earth.'

(Isaiah 49.1–6)

Like Christ told us in his Great Commission in Matthew 28.19–20 to go and spread the word that Jesus has risen and we can now have eternal life in him, God told us in Isaiah that we are to be God's witnesses. In fact, he repeats it many times just in case we might miss it. 'Did I not proclaim my purposes for you long ago? You are my witnesses – is there any other God? No! There is no other Rock – not one!' (Isaiah 44.8); 'I have put my words in your mouth and hidden you safely in my hand' (Isaiah 51.16).

Our purpose is steadfast: it has always been and will always be to be a witness. To tell people of what God has done for us, of what Christ has done for them, of what a life could be lived if they could accept God's love for them! We are to bring glory to his name in all the things we do. To testify of his love for us that has given us an identity in Christ. If you are a dreamer, then please dream. Dream of the many people who could come to know Christ because God called you on to the water to open your mouth and praise his name for all to hear!

YOU HAVE BEEN EQUIPPED!

God gives us resources (just read Matthew 25.14–30). Whether that be funds, talents, time, abilities or anything else, he has given them to us for the purpose of advancing the kingdom. He wants us to use them, hone them, invest them and better them so that we can bear fruit for many others to return to him. We are not given gifts to hide them in the dirt but rather to water them so they can grow.

If you can sing, then sing. If you can write, then write. If you can run, then run. If you can bake, then bake. Just make sure you don't put your **identity** in your talents; rather, keep it deeply rooted in the titles God has given you. Just make sure you don't put your **worth** in your talents; rather, make sure it is valued by the words God has spoken over you. Just make sure you don't put your entire **purpose** in your talents. It has always been and will always be to be a witness of God, which may look different in each season of your life. And let your unmoving goalpost be the words, 'Well done, my good and faithful servant' (Matthew 25.21).

If we are unfaithful, he remains faithful, for he cannot deny who he is.

(2 Timothy 2.13)

Chapter eight

TRUSTING GOD WITH YOUR FUTURE

So, we have reached the last chapter. Clearly, this is where I tell you that I am currently writing from my mansion in London, that you've most likely heard my singles if you've listened to Radio 1 for more than ten minutes, and that I can now say that God fulfilled all the dreams I had for myself, so he'll do it for you as well. Oh, and, 'You're doing great, sweetie!' and, 'Keep doing you and just be patient because God's got this!' Or . . .

I am currently writing from my home in Northern Ireland where I had to relocate to five years ago after a promoter ran off with all my money at a gig I was doing in Vietnam (not a joke). I got married three years ago to quite possibly the most gorgeous man on this earth, who loves Jesus and loves me – and I met him on a dating app called Bumble (also, not a joke). I am presently retching over this laptop because we found out a few weeks ago, before my son's first birthday, that we are pregnant again (again, not a joke). And I was rehired by the unnamed shop and am now once again working part-time selling overpriced skin-care lies (thankfully this *is* a joke). The point is, I couldn't be any further from the original dream. And I have never felt happier nor seen a season as beautiful as the one I am in now.

EXTRAORDINARY VS ORDINARY

A couple of years ago, I was crying to a friend about my career. I told her how I had spent my whole life pushing this dream and came so close, only to lose it all. How I then spent years trying to trust God and make it independently as an artist, only to never be able to make a living from it. And that now I just wasn't really feeling motivated to keep striving and was scared I was giving up.

She looked at me and said, with complete joy and sincerity, 'I know! What a beautiful season of life you are in! Praise God!'

I thought she must have zoned out for the last 20 minutes. I stared at her, waiting for her to admit her lack of listening skills, when she just smiled back at me. 'Leah, you have had a very long season of this . . .' She moved her hand up and down, creating a zigzag line. 'And so praise God he is giving you a season of this . . .' She pulled her hand across to draw an imaginary straight line. 'You fear your life has become boring, but you have never been happier and more content. He has given you a season of rest. A season of feeling safe. A season of the ordinary. Praise God!'

So here's what I want you to do, God helping you: Take your everyday, ordinary life – your sleeping, eating, going-to-work, and walking-around life – and place it before God as an offering. Embracing what God does for you is the best thing you can do for him. Don't become so well-adjusted to your culture that you fit into it without even thinking. Instead, fix your attention on God. You'll be changed from the inside out. Readily recognize what he wants from you, and quickly respond to it. Unlike the culture around you, always dragging you down to its level of immaturity, God brings the best out of you, develops well-formed maturity in you.

(Romans 12.1–2, *The Message*)

I burst out crying, because words have never seemed so true.

We have a culture of desiring an extraordinary life. But the fact is the original, perfect design from God for us consisted of us dancing around the garden of Eden, happy, in love, talking and walking with God. It was to be so stunningly simple. So exquisitely *normal*. To be our ordinary. Without striving, without disappointment, without feeling like a failure if we weren't constantly working on our big, unreachable dreams.

Right now, in our fallen world, we wouldn't be content with that, if we were honest, would we? Especially not as dreamers. We seek a great purpose. We want to be remembered for something great. We want to be a part of the incredible. These are all great things provided they are for God's glory. But in seeking this, are we giving ourselves permission to enjoy the simple and God-given treasures in life? Things like family, friendship, love and having hilarious people around that make us laugh when we should be crying? Like going to church, worshipping and enjoying learning about God and praising him? After all, a year in a pandemic, during which all these things were restricted, surely showed us how truly precious they all are to us. Have we forgotten that the incredible will be fulfilled in heaven when we are once again just spending our days walking and talking with God? There wouldn't be a need for extraordinary lives if the world had continued to sing the same tune as God.

The fact is that there was a fall. And therefore we need to get to work, witnessing and standing for Jesus in the dark places of the earth so more people can have these beautiful and perfect 'ordinary' lives in heaven for eternity. I realized in that moment with my friend that I had put a worldly desire for an extraordinary life on a pedestal. And a desire for the wondrous, 'ordinary', God-given blessings of life had unintentionally been stored in my brain as 'boring, normal things'. This warped vision of what makes an interesting and purposeful extraordinary life was causing me to weep over a failed career when I was actually in a season of happiness. A season for me to be content. A marriage, a beautiful son, back on a stage and singing into a microphone I had sung into as a teenager, leading worship with a church family who had walked all my seasons with me and crowded my living room when I experienced my deepest loss. I was home but with blessings now in abundance. And it wasn't a failure or a step back; it was a gift! Don't get me wrong – I had found so much joy in these things all along, but now this revelation gave me the freedom to enjoy them without feeling as if there was a big point on my to do list that I was ignoring and being lazy by not striving for.

It's not ungodly to desire an extraordinary life. The fact is we do live in a fallen world, and so there is a need for them still. The Bible is full of extraordinary lives. Lives that have enriched all of ours with words and promises of God. But as we mentioned before, these lives also endured a lot of pain and hardship. Pain and hardship do seem to go hand in hand with this kind of life, but for those who are so driven by the desire to see many people know and experience the love of God, their selfless, sacrificial lives can save so many. If you are one of these people, then I pray supernatural strength for you as you carry out your essential work on this fallen earth. And I pray that you have seasons of straight lines where you can enjoy the simple riches God originally designed for us.

Right now, many in the West are living in a time of relative peace. Our grandparents probably experienced a culture of simply wanting their family safe and being able to provide for them. We, however, are surrounded with people saying, 'You can be whatever you want to be.' This is very empowering but not entirely biblical. We are to offer our lives to God – every part of our lives. Of course, you have been equipped for amazing ministries, but don't value them as the world does. If you don't become a famous preacher and instead have led a church of 40 people, that is incredible! You have made God more famous, and that is our entire goal. Let us go against our culture and be dreamers who cultivate contentment.

I got to achieve so many things. I got to sing in arenas all around the world, to duet with extremely famous pop stars, to meet some of my industry heroes and to write and record an album with will.i.am that I was extremely proud of. But when it wasn't my own concerts, or when the music didn't get released, I felt I had achieved nothing. Six-year-old me would have been content with the dreams I did see come to pass, but for the adult me the goalpost kept moving. Even when I went on to release a record, 'INK', as an independent artist, performed 'Wolf Den' in the O2 arena and went on to sell out five of my own UK shows, discontentment started to creep in when I couldn't afford to live off the income I was getting. It has become clear to me that I was always going to be in want, no matter how far I went. Our culture would say that is ambition, but I think we often blur the lines of healthy ambition and discontentment.

Paul the apostle spoke profoundly about contentment when he was in prison. If he could do that, we can do it in our unforeseen ordinary lives.

> Not that I was ever in need, for I have learned how to be content with whatever I have. I know how to live on almost nothing or with everything. I have learned the secret of living in every situation, whether it is with a full stomach or empty, with plenty or little. For I can do everything through Christ, who gives me strength.
> (Philippians 4.11–13)

Be content in knowing that God sees the completed masterpiece and you are a thread in a tapestry that will be woven together carefully along with others to finish it for the glory of him. Every thread is treasured by him, and he wants you to also enjoy the simple and most beautiful things in life. Things like love, friends and family.

TRUSTING GOD'S CHARACTER

There are many facets to God's character, but through my journey one of many things I've learnt is that he is *faithful*. I don't know if you have ever sung the song 'Faithful One' by Brian Doerksen, but I've sung it nearly every week since I was about 12. We sang it at my sister's funeral, we sang it at my mum's wedding. And recently, as I embark on a new dream of writing worship songs, I released a cover of it, with Brian's blessing. Faithfulness is one of the most beautiful character traits of God. If someone is faithful, we deem them to be *trustworthy*.

All my exes cheated on me, so when I met my husband I took my time to trust him, but I soon began to see that the character trait of being faithful flowed out of him in every part of his life. He was faithful to his friends, his family, his mentee, his volunteer work, his job, church and God, and eventually I saw how fiercely faithful he was to me. Being faithful is who he is. I trust him with all my heart. And he is only human. He is, of course, capable of breaking that trust. But I don't believe he ever will.

Can I believe that God will not break my trust either? The Scriptures say that 'he remains faithful, for he cannot deny who he is' (2 Timothy 2.13). God is incapable of being unfaithful. Faithfulness is so fully his character. His *whole* character. The good parts of our character are only ever a fraction of his beautiful, wholesome character. He never gave up on his people. Even when they disobeyed him time and time again, he always remained faithful. This verse in 2 Timothy even starts with '*If we are unfaithful*', before continuing 'he remains faithful, for he cannot deny who he is' (italics added). Literally there is never a situation where God can or will be unfaithful to you.

AUDIENCE OF ONE

The term 'audience of one' is perhaps your 'Footprints in the sand', something you've heard so many times at cheesy youth events that it makes you cringe. But as I was writing a worship song this year with my friend and Christian artist Nathan Jess, we came across a verse in Luke 10 and were struck by Christ's words. If people were to ask, 'Where is Leah?' I would love someone to reply, 'She's at Jesus' feet.'

These are the words that Christ says to Martha, who is busying herself with life tasks and hasn't seized this wondrous moment, '"Martha, Martha," the Lord answered, "you are worried and upset about many things, but *few things are needed – or indeed only one*. Mary has chosen what is better, and it will not be taken away from her"' (italics added).

I know we have work to do. I know that we have to keep moving in order to advance the kingdom of God. But if we could do everything from the spiritual stance of sitting at Jesus' feet,

As Jesus and his disciples were on their way, he came to a village where a woman named Martha opened her home to him. She had a sister called Mary, who sat at the Lord's feet listening to what he said. But Martha was distracted by all the preparations that had to be made. She came to him and asked, 'Lord, don't you care that my sister has left me to do the work by myself? Tell her to help me!'

'Martha, Martha,' the Lord answered, 'you are worried and upset about many things, but few things are needed – or indeed only one. Mary has chosen what is better, and it will not be taken away from her.'

(Luke 10.38–42, NIV)

worshipping, resting in his presence as the children of God, listening to his every word, reading his every word in Scripture and praying about all things, imagine how fruitful we would be. Imagine how few worries we would have. Sitting at Jesus' feet is not wasted time, time not working on making your dreams come true. Christ said it himself that 'Mary has chosen what is better, and it will not be taken away from her'.

I pray that you would rest at Jesus' feet and leave all your dreams there. I pray that when anyone asks where you are, your heart would be so full of worship, of trust, of love for your Jesus that they would have to respond that you are where you always are – at his feet. That you would enjoy your precious life, disregard discontentment and worldly ambition, and choose what is better.

At your feet (written by Leah McFall and Nathan Jess)

There was a moment
When I missed your voice.
I was distracted
By all of life's noise.
I couldn't see
That few things are needed, or really there's only one.

I wanna stay here at your feet.
I wanna stay when the world is calling me.

I was invited
To rest here with you
In a holy aroma
As you tend my wounds.
Now I can see
Few things are needed, or Jesus, there's only one.

I wanna stay here at your feet.
I wanna stay when the world is calling me.

Should anyone ask,
If they can't find me,
This is where I'll be.

CLOSING

My life has changed dramatically in the past few years. And, ironically, they are the only years I have had that have been relatively drama free. I have been worried up until now that you might find where I am in life disappointing and utterly uninspiring. So *ordinary*. But God reminded my spirit that if it had been the first scenario then perhaps your focus would have become 'the dream' again, and not the 'dream giver'. Seeing someone achieve their personal goal can make us driven to achieve our own (which is great provided it doesn't cut God and his timing out of the picture). Or perhaps it would have encouraged you to stay with the 'original dream' that you had for your life and would not encourage you to free yourself up for

God to give you a new one. A fresh one. A more timely one for the season of life you are in now. Perhaps, 'You have stayed at this mountain long enough. It is time to break camp and move on' (Deuteronomy 1.6–7). Or perhaps God wants to simply remind your heart that the goal is always going on the journey *with* him. It's time to learn or relearn to trust the trustworthy one and to deepen your relationship with him.

Whatever the reason, I am humbly admitting to being without an answer as to what the destination of our future years will look like for you or for me, but I am fiercely encouraging us all to dream of what our hearts could look like before we get there. 'But seek first his kingdom and his righteousness, and all these things will be given to you as well' (Matthew 6.33, NIV). Committed, thankful and content hearts that seek God's kingdom first and remain in the vine will be refreshed. Hearts that are quick to trust through fear, disappointment, doubt and confusion. Hearts that speak kindness to ourselves and to others. Hearts that recognize the language of Satan and refuse to speak it. Hearts that know so profoundly we are the ones whom Jesus loves. Hearts that are quick to obey and to set up altars to be reminded of how God has been faithful in the past to cheer us on into the future. Hearts that trust the one who can be trusted. Hearts that place their dreams into God's hands.

I mentioned a destination of our dreams there, but to be truthful I believe that there isn't one. Not only because we are human and would keep moving the goalpost of that dream, but ultimately because our destination is heaven. And on the journey here on this imperfect earth there will be many more seasons to come for us, seasons of high highs and low lows that our journeys have been skilfully equipping us for without our knowing.

I hope that my words have encouraged you to look back and see what a way God has brought you. I hope that these pages have made you fall in love with the words in Scripture that God has been singing over you since before you were born.

I pray that we all can rest and know that our God loves his children and has dreams for us more beautiful than we could draw for ourselves. As his children, may we ask him to ignite fresh dreams within us that image his own. Dreams that glorify him for the purpose of advancing the kingdom. And as we commit those dreams into our heavenly Father's hands, may we fall back freely in a childlike trust into the arms of the one who cannot deny who he is, and therefore will always faithfully catch us.

Lord, I pray for these dreamers. Thank you for the mighty plans you have for them. Thank you for the people who will come to know you through their lives and ministries. Thank you for your children here, whom you love more deeply than they could ever imagine. May they enjoy many straight lines as they use their gifts and talents to seek first the kingdom of

*God on earth. Protect their minds. Protect their hearts. Deepen their faith. Deepen their **trust**. Keep them and their dreams deeply rooted in your vine.*

Amen.

Bibliography

Greig, Pete (2007), *God on Mute* (Eastbourne: Kingsway Publications).

Lewis, C. S. (1955), *The Magician's Nephew* (London: The Bodley Head).

Meyer, Joyce (2008), *Battlefield of the Mind* (London: Hodder & Stoughton).

Moore, Beth (2007), *Breaking Free* (Nashville, TN: Broadman & Holman).

Copyright acknowledgements

FORM IS A SPIRITUAL FORMATION IMPRINT OF SPCK

As well as being an award-winning publisher, SPCK is the oldest Anglican mission agency in the world.

Our mission is to lead the way in creating books and resources that help everyone to make sense of faith.

Will you partner with us to put good books into the hands of prisoners, great assemblies in front of schoolchildren, help create small groups resources for our Home Groups website and reach out to people who have not yet been touched by the Christian faith?

To donate, please visit www.spckpublishing.co.uk/donate or call our friendly fundraising team on 020 7592 3900.